CAPE PLAYS

THE FARM

DAVID STOREY

THE FARM

JONATHAN CAPE
THIRTY BEDFORD SQUARE LONDON

FIRST PUBLISHED 1973
© 1973 BY DAVID STOREY

JONATHAN CAPE LTD
30 BEDFORD SQUARE, LONDON WC1

ISBN Hardback 0 224 00870 6
Paperback 0 224 00872 2

PRINTED IN GREAT BRITAIN
BY EBENEZER BAYLIS & SON LTD
THE TRINITY PRESS, WORCESTER AND LONDON
ON PAPER MADE BY JOHN DICKINSON & CO. LTD
BOUND BY G. & J. KITCAT LTD, LONDON

CHARACTERS

WENDY

JENNIFER

BRENDA

SLATTERY

MRS SLATTERY

ALBERT

ARTHUR

ACT ONE

The lounge, or living-room, of a farmhouse: amply proportioned and of some antiquity. Casement-type windows and a more recently constructed french window look out, at the rear, to the garden.

A large stone fireplace occupies the wall stage right; a door, matching the shoulder-height wood-panelling, occupies the centre of the wall stage left. The furniture is of generous proportions: a chintz-covered three-piece suite, an oak dresser with brass-work, an oak sideboard. There's a bookcase, well stocked, and a desk set against the wall, covered in papers, files, etc. The place has a spacious, easy-going atmosphere, earthy, plain, over-used: the feeling of a burrow, stained, familiar, caverned-out. One or two framed prints (old) hang on the wall.

WENDY, *a young, independent, perhaps rather severe-looking woman of thirty-three is reading in one of the easy chairs. She's got a pile of books on the floor beside her, a cup of coffee on a small table, and cigarettes and a lighter. A tray with a coffee pot, milk jug, etc., stands on the sideboard.*

Door closes off: low whistle.

JENNIFER *comes in the door: well, not ostentatiously, dressed, she's slightly younger than* WENDY. *Attractive. She has on a coat with a fur collar, and a pair of gloves. She carries no bag.*

JENNY (*looks round; greets her*). Sweets ...
WENDY. Lovey ... (*Having looked up, resumes her reading.*)
JENNY. Freezing ...
WENDY. How'd it go?
JENNY. Usual ... (*Takes off her gloves: warms hands.*)
    Dad not in?

7

(WENDY *shakes head, still reading.*)
Mum?

WENDY. Out.

(*Banging overhead.* JENNY *looks up, shivers from the cold, then takes off coat. Goes to coffee jug.*)

JENNY. Anything in here for me?

WENDY. Might be.

JENNY. Hardly ...

WENDY. Oh, dear. (*Still reading.*)

JENNY. Hardly any.

WENDY. See what you've been missing, love.

(JENNY *picks up* WENDY'S *cup: pours a drop of coffee. Banging overhead: hammer blows.*)

JENNY. What 'you been doing, Sweets?

WENDY. Nothing.

JENNY. Why do you use lipstick in the house?

WENDY. What? (*Looks up: first look of interest.*)

(JENNY *holds up the cup.*)

JENNY. Can't you get that stuff that doesn't come off?

WENDY. Dunno.

JENNY. Expecting anybody, are you?

WENDY. No.

JENNY (*having tasted it, puts cup down*). Don't think I'll drink it after all.

WENDY. Sick?

JENNY (*groans, murmurs in affirmative*). You in a rotten mood as well?

(WENDY *reading: hums assent, singsong. Banging comes from overhead.*)

JENNY (*looks up*). What's she up to?

WENDY. Placards.

JENNY. Placards?

WENDY. Notices.

JENNY. Who for?

WENDY. Exhorting herself to rise and shine. (*Looks up at* JENNY.) See the one she put on the old man's table? ... 'The shortest distance between two people is a smile.'
(*They laugh.*
Pause.)

JENNY. Mother and the old man out together?

WENDY. On her own. (*Looks up at clock, above fireplace.*)

JENNY (*picks up book from pile*). How many of these do you get through in a week?

WENDY. Dunno.

JENNY. On average.

WENDY. No idea.

JENNY(*picks up another*). Why do you never read books by men?

WENDY. Dunno.

JENNY (*examines book. Directly, since* WENDY *goes on reading:*) Brenda's been writing one for years ... I hate to think what she's putting down ... Do you think it's got anything to do with us?

WENDY. Doubt it. (*Still reads.*)

JENNY. Got a light?
(*She takes a cigarette from* WENDY's *packet.* WENDY *flicks the lighter.*)
Have you seen this restaurant they've got? Top of an office block or something ... 'Poulet aux Galette de Mais.' Everything they've got is chicken ... 'Chaudfroid de Poulet Yorkshire' sounded rather good.

WENDY. What's his name?

JENNY. Harold.

WENDY. Do you call him that?

JENNY. Why not?

WENDY. Dunno ...
(*JENNY wanders round the room. Then:*)

JENNY. I read a book the other day by a woman who'd been married fourteen times.

9

(WENDY *goes on reading.*)

You get married again, then, Wendy?

WENDY. Think I might?

JENNY. Only one round here who's tried.

WENDY. Alus Mother.

JENNY. Alus Mam.

WENDY. Hear her extra-mural course is leading her into very deep waters.

JENNY. What?

WENDY. Lecturer in sociology, I hear, is a disenchanted man ... Divorced his wife two years ago ... An era of disillusionment has been lightened by our ma.

JENNY. Good grief.

WENDY. Introduced, I fear, an element of hope.

JENNY. Who told you?

WENDY. Last night. Came into my room ... asked me if I'd mind ... Hearing all about this man, I mean ... Apparently he's only forty-four ...

JENNY. Good God.

(WENDY *reads.*)

Would you marry a man who's forty-four?

WENDY. Dunno.

JENNY. How old was Bryan?

WENDY. Twenty-two.

JENNY. How old is he now?

WENDY (*still reading*). Dunno ...

JENNY. Forty-four's quite old, I reckon ... (*Considers it.*) Would Bryan have suited me, you think?

WENDY (*reading*). Had his eye on you, you know.

JENNY. Really! ... Never told me!

WENDY. We'd only been married about six months.

JENNY. Perseverance.

(JENNY, *having sat down during this dialogue, gets up: wanders off towards the window.*)

(*Gazing out*) He's not this man with a black moustache?

WENDY (*reading*). That's right.

JENNY. Saw her with him in town, the other day ... Thought he was a salesman ... looked innocuous to me.

WENDY. Not up to the psychologist, you think?

JENNY. Rather fancied him, I think, meself. Mother went off him when I asked her what colour ties he wore.

WENDY. Always resented growing old ... I think she feels we're catching up ... would like to share our effervescence ... (*Bangs overhead.*) A little longer ... (*Looks up.*) I think she's coming down.

(WENDY *goes back to her book, intently.*

JENNY *hastily picks one up: crashing on stairs, off.*

BRENDA *comes in: fierce girl of twenty-three, in jeans and sweater.*)

BRENDA. Have you seen a box of screws ... S'got a yellow label on one end ... You're back.

JENNY. Been back for hours.

BRENDA. I saw you in the drive. Mauling that man from the plastics factory.

JENNY. Not true.

BRENDA. I've got two eyes ... Half-strangled him, she did. Be glad to get back to his plastic pots.

JENNY. At least I kiss the man goodnight ... I don't shake hands and slap him on the back.

BRENDA. I've been meaning to tell you this for some considerable time. You're nothing but a whore.

JENNY. I am.

BRENDA. She's another. God help me if I ever turn out like one of you.

WENDY. What're you screwing up, then, Brenda?

BRENDA. What?

WENDY. Bedroom. (*Gestures up.*)

BRENDA. I'm fastening a bookshelf to my wall.

WENDY. Why don't you buy one?

BRENDA. I don't buy one, because I'm quite capable of making one myself … It's as simple … (*To* JENNY) and as reasonable … as that.

WENDY (*puts down her book*). Do you remember when Brenda here was a little girl?

JENNY. Fastened Father in the lavatory, she did.

BRENDA. I did not.

JENNY. Oooh!

BRENDA. *Arthur* locked the door — but hadn't the courage to admit it … As a result I took the blame myself.

WENDY. Poor old Arthur.

BRENDA. Poor old Arthur! … Poor old Arthur got out of it — I thought — rather well. Poor old Arthur gets out of everything, in my view, rather well.

WENDY. You'd never think she was the youngest sister.

JENNY. You wouldn't.

WENDY. You'd imagine all that militancy to come out of someone who'd been exposed — prematurely — to all the perverse vicissitudes of life which we — Jenny and myself — have encountered virtually alone …

JENNY. Unaided.

BRENDA. I've never been protected.

JENNY. Too gracious to admit it …

WENDY. Always has been.

BRENDA. Have you seen my screws?

(*They laugh.*)

WENDY. Looked in Mother's bedroom. Always picking something up …

BRENDA. If you're trying to draw me into that, I better warn you … For one day, I've had enough. (*Starts searching round the room.*)

(WENDY *returns to her book.*
JENNY *lights another cigarette.*)

WENDY. I can't see why you can't use a nail instead.

BRENDA. If you ever acquired any *useful* information—you would realize that a nail breaks up the plaster. It also, after a while—*drops out.*

(*Outer door bangs: gruff coughs, clearing of throat, etc.*)

WENDY. Specialist's here. Ask him ... Bound to tell you. (*To* JENNY) Put your cigarette out, girl. Look out.

(BRENDA *goes on searching.*

JENNY *composes herself, stubbing cigarette.*

WENDY *stubs hers; sets herself more firmly in her chair, still reading.*

SLATTERY *comes in. He's a stocky, well-built man, sixty-five.*)

SLATTERY. Evening. (*Looks round: suspicious, wary.*)

WENDY *and* JENNY (*together*). Evening, Father.

SLATTERY. Thought some of you would have been in bed.

JENNY. Here, you mean, or somewhere else?

SLATTERY (*examines* JENNY *for a while. Then:*) Your mother in, then, is she?

WENDY. Out.

SLATTERY. Find me slippers for meself, 'spect.

BRENDA. I'll get them for you.

SLATTERY. Give ought for a cup of tea ...

WENDY. That's coffee.

SLATTERY. Oh, well ... Do without as soon as ought ... Where you been tonight, then, Jenny?

JENNY. Out, Father. Looking for a feller.

SLATTERY. Aye. Well ... (*Eyes her for a moment. Sits.*) Been up at top end, meself ... Bloody stack's blown down ... Blown down! Not a drop of bloody wind. Shoved it up any old bloody fashion. Don't go up meself you'll get nowt done ... Bloody labour force ... I ne'er see much bloody labour ... As for bloody force ... (*Looks from one to the other: they take no notice.*) Been bloody smoking. Don't worry, I can tell ... Be dead afore you're fifty. I'm telling you. Won't listen. Bloody cancer. (*Coughs.*)

(BRENDA *brings his slippers.*)

Mother's out at college, is she?

BRENDA. Yep.

SLATTERY. O'der I get, less I understand. Fathered three and married one: I know less now than when I started.

WENDY. Could be said of all of us, I think.

SLATTERY. Thy's only one life ... Make best on it while thy's got the chance ... If they were all like you, where would you get to, then? Eh? Nowt living as us call a human kind ... nowt but bloody animals and trees ... Can tell you your trouble for a bloody start.

WENDY. I'm listening ... (*Looks up from book.*)

SLATTERY. Thinks I'm bloody daft ... (*To* BRENDA) Prick up their bloody ears one day. Mark my words.

JENNY (*sits on the arm beside him*). Nay. Come on. Out with it ... What's our trouble, Dad?

SLATTERY. Nay ... (*Mollified*) I think if I married again I'd bring up half a dozen bloody goats ... Bloody hosses ... Damn sight more rewarding ... Still ...

(*They wait, all turned towards him.*)

I've seen nowt as daft as your bloody mother ... trying to learn at night-school all she's known for fifty bloody years ... and from men half her bloody age at that ... learnt nowt but what they've read inside a book ... God Christ! ... Nay. I've said enough ...

WENDY. Maybe we should've all been sons.

SLATTERY. Aye ... Well, example thy's had, I shouldn't think you'd get very much from that.

(*They're silent.*)

Nay, well. I just hate to see something going to rot.

JENNY. *What's* going to rot?

SLATTERY. When your mother was your age she'd had all four of you.

WENDY. You think if we all had children you'd feel a bit easier about us, Dad?

SLATTERY. I'm saying nowt ... If a woman can't have babbies when she's young, I don't know what else she can have. I don't ... Comes naturally as bloody breathing ... Your own nature's enough to tell you that.

JENNY. You've lived on a farm too long, old lad.

SLATTERY. I've lived next to God's good earth. That's where I've lived ... Still ... Aye.

BRENDA. In any case, I'm leaving. I thought I'd mentioned that.

SLATTERY. You've mentioned it. You've mentioned it two or three times, as I reckon it, afore ... No doubt you'll mention it again.

WENDY. Bed for me ... (*Yawns. Gets up.*)

SLATTERY. You want to think on what I've bloody said.

WENDY. Don't worry. Bear it all in mind. (*Kisses his forehead.*)

SLATTERY. Off to work tomorrow?

WENDY. I am ...

SLATTERY. Your mother's told you, has she? ... Your brother's coming.

WENDY. Well, *I've* been told ... Don't know about the others.

JENNY (*shakes her head*). I didn't know.

BRENDA. Neither did I.

JENNY. What's he coming for?

SLATTERY. Nay. Don't ask me ought. You better ask your mother ... Cadging round her, I shouldn't be surprised ...

JENNY. Doesn't usually forewarn us. (*To* WENDY) Usually collapses on the doorstep, unannounced.

SLATTERY. Going to give us one more of his surprises, then.

Can't bloody wait for it meself ... (*To* JENNY) You off to bed as well, then, are you?

JENNY. Think I might ... Had a rotten night. Feel sick.

SLATTERY. Don't worry. It'll all go bad ... It rots away inside ... And bloody smoking doesn't help.

JENNY. Aye. Well. Too late to worry now. (*Kisses his cheek.*) See you in the morning, love.

SLATTERY. 'Spect so. If you're up in time.

JENNY. What time's he coming, then?

SLATTERY. Don't ask me. His own time as usual, I expect ... God's *great* bloody gift ... Be grateful whatever time it happens.

WENDY. Aye. Well.

SLATTERY. Drops like bloody manna ... The usual arrangement, I expect.

BRENDA. There's no need to be bitter.

SLATTERY. Nay, I'm not bloody bitter ... I've had every damn reason enough to *feel* embittered ... But I'm bloody not. I can tell you that.

JENNY. Well, up to bed-for-cheers, for me ... (*Collects her coat and gloves. She goes.*)

WENDY (*to* SLATTERY). I'll make you a pot of tea, if you like, before I go.

SLATTERY. S'all right. I'll wait up for your mother ...

WENDY. Ah, well ... Brenda ...

BRENDA. Yeh ... Good night.

(WENDY *picks up her books, her cigarettes and lighter: goes.* SLATTERY, *after a pause, gets up. He goes to the oak dresser.*)

SLATTERY. Aye. Well ... Reckon a drop of this won't go astray.

(*Gets out whisky: pours an ample measure.*)

BRENDA. I thought you'd been rationed, Dad.

SLATTERY. Had half a drop this morning, love ... Means I

can have t'other half on it right now ... (*Drinks.*) By go
... What the bloody doctor ordered ... Don't split, now.
Don't let on.

BRENDA. You know why you drink so much now, don't you?

SLATTERY. Aye. Well. A've a bloody good idea.

BRENDA. Don't want to hear about it, I suppose.

SLATTERY. I don't give a damn. Not one road nor another.

(BRENDA *doesn't respond.*

SLATTERY *looks across.*)

Sithee ... know where I was when I was half your bloody
age? (*Holds up two hands.*) On my knees, twelve hours of
the day, scrattin' bloody 'taties.

BRENDA. Ah, well. You haven't done so bad.

SLATTERY. I haven't ... Sat down on me backside half the
bloody day—like somebody I could mention—you'd
hear some bloody complaints. You would.

BRENDA. Everything we have here ... (*Gestures round, looking*)
... has been gained at the expense of other people.

SLATTERY. Aye. (*Pours another ample one.*)

BRENDA. That's your answer, I think, to everything.

SLATTERY. Aye. Almost. (*Drinks.*) Like your bloody mother,
you ... Two of a kind ... One good thing about your
mother: she got it late in life, and not afore.

BRENDA. Not afore she was disillusioned, then.

SLATTERY. Your mother's not disillusioned ... She's just not
got much bloody common sense ... No great failing, that,
in my book ... She's got a heart as big as that bloody door
... It'll alus see her through.

BRENDA. It'll not see her through all that whisky, I can tell
you.

SLATTERY. It'll see her through the next ten years or more ...
As for me. Like petrol to an engine, this: I couldn't run
a day wi'out.

(BRENDA *watches him for a while.*)

BRENDA. Your trouble is ... You see me ... and Jenny. And our Wendy ... Like some sort of primeval cattle. Cows.

SLATTERY. Nay, coos know what they're bloody after ... I don't think any one of you know one end of a man from bloody t'other ... Look at Wendy. Married sixteen months ... Then leaves ... A bloody doctor. God Christ: I'd almost marry the man meself ... As for bloody Jenny. By God: I've heard of flitting from flower to flower ... she never even stops to rest. (*Drinks.*)

BRENDA. I pity you more than anything else.

SLATTERY. A thought thy bloody would ... (*To himself*) Have another ... Aye. All right. I will.

BRENDA. You're nothing but an animal yourself ... All these years ... We've tried to think of you as something else.

SLATTERY. Aye ... (*Drinks up.*) By go. Man that invented this goes very high. In my bloody book ... He does. Knew summat about human nature ... Didn't get his notion from reading bloody books ...

(MRS SLATTERY *comes in: a pleasant, cheery woman, companionable, not easily overwhelmed. She's dressed in a warm coat and has a practical woollen hat and gloves.*)

MRS SLATTERY. What's this? I can hear it down the drive.

SLATTERY. Thy bloody lasses. Don't blame me. Swallowed a gramophone needle at some time i' their lives: I don't know when.

MRS SLATTERY. Them or you? (*Smiles at* BRENDA.) Just look at this ... (*Goes to the bottle.*) You've not had more than you're supposed to have?

SLATTERY. Nay, what does a man who's never had a drop know about how much you're supposed to have? God Christ.

MRS SLATTERY. I should think the doctor's had a drop or two ... *In his time.*

SLATTERY. He's bloody tee-total. Told me so himself ...

18

'Come off it, Joe,' he said, 'and I can promise you another ten years at least.' 'Ten years without?' I said. 'I mun drop down deard now if I thought thy meant it.'

MRS SLATTERY (*to* BRENDA). I shall have to give up these evenings ... He's like a child ... Can't be left alone for two minutes.

SLATTERY (*finishes his glass*). No need to worry ... Our Brenda's been setting me to rights ... Have me out i' the cowsheds if she had the chance, not tucked up warm in bed ... Where's thy been all this time, then? ... Woman thy age ...

MRS SLATTERY. A woman my age, surely, doesn't have to account for where she's been?

SLATTERY. A woman thy age ought to have more bloody common sense ... Gallivanting out ... All right. I'll say nowt else. I know my bloody place. Should do. All these years.

BRENDA. Self-pity ... It's the one commodity he's never short of.

(SLATTERY *looks to* MRS SLATTERY *to intervene.*)

MRS SLATTERY. Nay, I don't want to intrude, love ... You argue all you want ... I can tell you: I've had quite a few hours of it down there ... I used to think I'd got *some* things *half*-worked out ... as it is, the more I listen, the less I seem to know ...

SLATTERY. You know a damn sight more than half those silly sods down there ... I'm surprised you give 'em two minutes of your bloody time ... Psychiatry? ... By bloody hell ... Gi'e me ten bloody minutes wi' 'em in top end and I'll psychiatrize the bloody lot.

MRS SLATTERY (*to* BRENDA). Look ... hand's shaking ... I've got a splitting head ... Has Wendy gone to bed?

SLATTERY. She has ... Be up there all bloody day if she got half a chance ... Surprised she troubles to get out at all ...

Up at bloody half-past four meself ... seven days a week, fifty-two weeks i' the year ... fo'ty-five bloody years ... (*To* BRENDA) How's that for a bloody life?

BRENDA. Can't beat it.

MRS SLATTERY. Is Jenny in, then, love, as well?

BRENDA. She is.

MRS SLATTERY. Can lock up, then ...

SLATTERY. Been telling her ... and *them* ... it's not men they've gotten wrong ... It's *hers' en* that never comes up to scratch.

MRS SLATTERY. Oh, well. I think I've had enough ... I'm too tired to listen to any more tonight ... (*To* BRENDA) All goes past me. (*To* SLATTERY) They seem to know what they're on about.

SLATTERY. If they do, they keep it to their bloody s'ens ... Mek a bloody secret of it, I can tell you ... And we'll have another bloody load tomorrow. (*Toasts.*) God's bloody gift to the bone bloody idle. (*Finds his glass empty, puts it down.*) Eat me bloody food ... sleep i' me bloody beds ... Seen nowt like it ... Get a job, she will, one day ... Freeten us all to bloody death ... (*To* BRENDA) Gi'e us all a bloody shock.

MRS SLATTERY. Time he was in bed.

SLATTERY. I'm going. Don't worry. Another hour down here and I'm going to have nowt left ... Are you coming up?

MRS SLATTERY. I'll be up in a couple of minutes ... I'll just lock up.

SLATTERY. Lock up? There's nowt to lock up here ... You ask her ... Gi'e it all away, if she had a chance ... (*To* BRENDA) Gi'e it all away, you know, and they'd still come back for more ... (*Sees* MRS SLATTERY'*s look.*) Aye ... Well ... (*Shakes his head and goes.*)

MRS SLATTERY. Ah, well ... Another day over, love ... At times you think it'll never end. (*Goes to put bottle away:*

20

BRENDA *picks up glass.*) What've you been up to, then?

BRENDA. Nothing.

MRS SLATTERY. Here. I'll cope with these ...

SLATTERY (*reappearing*). Forgot to say good night.

BRENDA. Oh ... Good night.

SLATTERY (*looks over at* MRS SLATTERY). See you in a minute, then?

MRS SLATTERY. Don't worry ... I shan't be long.

SLATTERY. Aye ... (*Looks over at* BRENDA, *looks at* MRS SLATTERY.) Good night. (*He goes.*)

BRENDA. I don't know how you put up with it.

MRS SLATTERY. I think he'll be all right.

BRENDA. All these years ... (*Waits.*) Didn't you ever run away?

MRS SLATTERY. Run away?

BRENDA. Before you had our Wendy ...

MRS SLATTERY. Run away from what?

BRENDA. Nay, if you don't know ... I don't think I could begin to tell you.

MRS SLATTERY. Nay, love ... (*Brushes back* BRENDA'*s hair.*) Your father's not as bad as that.

BRENDA. He's contemptible.

MRS SLATTERY. Nay, love ... He's your father ... I can't change how you feel ... But I wish you wouldn't say it ... Not here ... Not to me.

BRENDA. I just feel so bloody sorry for you, Mam.

MRS SLATTERY. You're making something out of nothing, girl ... Just because he drinks ...

BRENDA. Drinks ... Do you think if he didn't drink he'd be any better? If anything he'd be a damn sight worse.

MRS SLATTERY. Nay, well I don't want to hear it, love ...

BRENDA. Did you love him when you married him?

MRS SLATTERY. I suppose I must have done ... It's not something you care to talk about. Not really.

BRENDA. Why not?

MRS SLATTERY. Well ... I never think of it like that.

BRENDA. How do you think of it, then?

MRS SLATTERY. I don't know ... I was only twenty when I married him ... He was very much the sort of man, you know, who, if he saw a thing, went out and got it ... There don't seem to be many people like that nowadays ...

BRENDA. Nowadays?

MRS SLATTERY. Well, I don't know ... Everybody seems so uncertain ... The ones who do seem confident ... you'd dismiss as stupid, I expect.

BRENDA. I don't know. It depends what they're confident about.

MRS SLATTERY. Yes ... Well. (*Pause.*) I better get to bed.

BRENDA. I'll lock up for you, if you like.

MRS SLATTERY. Yes. All right, then, love ... (*Kisses her.*) Good night.

BRENDA. 'Night.

> (MRS SLATTERY *goes.*
>
> BRENDA *looks round, aimlessly, at the room. Then she goes to the dresser and pours a drink herself. Takes a deep drink: swallows; savours it, closing eyes.*
>
> *Tapping at window.*)

What ...

> (*Startled, goes across: pulls back curtain on french window; peers out.*)

Albert? (*Listens to someone talking the other side.*) Go round ... No ... Round ... *Round* ... Oh. All right. (*Unlocks the french window.*)

> (ALBERT *comes in, a young workman, dressed in jeans and zip jacket.*)

ALBERT. Freezing ... Been out there half an hour.

BRENDA. Why didn't you come in?

22

ALBERT. Saw your father ... Then your mother came ...
Have your sisters gone to bed?

BRENDA. Here ... Have a drop of that. (*Hands him her glass.*)

ALBERT (*sips it*). Crumbs ... You drink that a lot?

BRENDA. Sometimes ... (*Takes it back.*) Feel any better?

ALBERT. Nearly gave up ... walked up and down for half an
hour ... set off back ... Do you think they'll come back
down?

BRENDA. Don't think so.

ALBERT. Better leave the window open.

BRENDA. Not likely. Freeze to death. (*Closes it.*)

ALBERT. Can't stay long ... Thought I'd just pop up. (*Prowls
around, uncertain.*)

BRENDA. Here ... If anybody comes I'll leave it on the latch
... You'll hear them. Anybody moves in this house half
the woodwork creaks ... Here. Sit down.

ALBERT. Must think I'm mad.

BRENDA. What?

ALBERT. Coming here like this.

BRENDA. Not really ... (*Watching him.*) How did you get
here, then?

ALBERT. Bike ... (*Looks to the window.*) I left it by that hedge.

BRENDA. Lights on: pedals ready ...

ALBERT. No ... (*Laughs.*) Not as bad as that.

BRENDA. What've you been doing, then, tonight?

ALBERT. Got home from work ... Mucked around ... I rang
you up, as a matter of fact.

BRENDA. Tonight?

ALBERT. Earlier on ...

BRENDA. They never told me.

ALBERT. Well, it was your sister answered.

BRENDA. What d'you say?

ALBERT. Nothing ... I put it down ... (*Laughs.*) Don't know
why.

23

BRENDA. Without telling her you wanted me?

ALBERT. I didn't say anything, as a matter of fact ... When I heard her voice ... I don't know why ... Heard her say the number ... (*Looks up.*) Put the phone down.

BRENDA (*studies him. Then:*) Are you the same with other people as you are with me?

ALBERT. Dunno ... Never been in a house like this before.

BRENDA. What's the matter with the house?

ALBERT. Dunno ... So old ...

BRENDA. I come down to your house, don't I?

ALBERT. Yeh.

BRENDA. What's the difference, then? People live in here: people live in your house.

ALBERT. You can walk right through ours and not notice it's even there.

BRENDA. I'd have thought you'd have despised it ... Not been afraid of it ... Not run away.

ALBERT. I haven't run away.

BRENDA. No.

ALBERT. I'm here, then, aren't I?

BRENDA. How many times have you been up here before?

ALBERT. Once or twice.

BRENDA. How many?

ALBERT. Half a dozen.

BRENDA. And never knocked?

    (ALBERT *doesn't answer.*)

    You can't be frightened of the house. I don't believe it ... Have another drink.

ALBERT. I better not.

BRENDA. Not if you're riding back, you mean?

    (*Pause.*)

ALBERT. You're always laughing, you know.

BRENDA. Laughing?

ALBERT. Scoffing.

BRENDA. Scoffing?

ALBERT. I've cycled up here, haven't I?

BRENDA. Why are you so frightened, then, of Wendy?

ALBERT. I'm not frightened ... Well. All right.

BRENDA. And Jenny? ... Are you frightened, then, of her?

ALBERT. Why don't you women ever get married?

BRENDA. Wendy has been married.

ALBERT. About two years, by what I reckon.

BRENDA. Who've you been talking to?

ALBERT. Nobody ... Just asked around.

BRENDA. I'll tell you anything you want to know ... Or are you frightened of me as well?

(*Pause.*)

ALBERT. Don't think so.

BRENDA. Why not?

ALBERT. Dunno ... Still a bit of hope, I 'spect.

BRENDA. They're only just over thirty. For goodness sake. How old are you?

ALBERT. Twenty ... Twenty-one ... Nearly ... What's that? (*Leaps up.*)

BRENDA. Nothing ... S'always creaking ... At night you can almost hear it breathe ... Like being inside a person ... I'm only two years older. It can't be age.

ALBERT. What do your sisters do?

BRENDA. They teach ...

(ALBERT *moves round, uneasy.*)

ALBERT. I came up here—one day last summer ... Just after I'd met you ... It wa'n half hot. It took me over an hour to cycle up ... I went by along that road down yonder ... I don't know whether I meant to stop ... I looked over the hedge and saw them sitting on the lawn ... One of them was smoking ... Had her hair cut short.

BRENDA. Wendy ...

ALBERT. The other one was reading something from a book

... Couldn't hear what it was ... just the voice ... Wendy started laughing. Leaning back ...

BRENDA. Must have put you off.

ALBERT. I just felt she'd laugh at ought ... anything that took her fancy ... Must have settled it right then ... Couldn't understand it ...

BRENDA. What?

ALBERT. Dunno ... I came back about ten minutes later ... Your mother—must have been your mother ... She'd come out and joined them ... All three of them were laughing ... Don't know what it was.

BRENDA. You make it sound like a bloody harem.

ALBERT. My sister got married when she was seventeen ... Got three kiddies now ... She's not much o'der than you ... hasn't been back home since the day she wed ... not for long enough you'd notice ...

BRENDA. Well?

ALBERT. Tisn't as if your dad's an invalid or ought ... or your mother needs looking after.

BRENDA. It seems unnatural?

ALBERT. Unnatural ...

BRENDA. Not quite right?

ALBERT. Dunno ... I've never heard of it afore.

BRENDA. Lots of things, I imagine, you've never heard about before.

ALBERT. What's your brother do?

BRENDA. Nothing.

ALBERT. Hasn't he got a job?

BRENDA. He's had a job ... What he's got at present I haven't a clue.

ALBERT. How's he earn his living?

BRENDA. No idea.

ALBERT. Does your dad pay him something, then?

BRENDA. Shouldn't think so.

(ALBERT *looks around the room again, mystified.*)

ALBERT. My father's lost his job ... Don't think I told you.

BRENDA. No.

ALBERT. Don't think he's bothered ... Not while *I'm* working ... My mother's the one who frets ... They've taken a liking, you know, to you ... My father's never got over you coming down to see him.

BRENDA. That's not why he lost his job?

ALBERT. No ... No ... Two or three hundred been set off ... They're closing down an entire shop ... My turn next. Then we'll be all right ... Nobody's ever come down to see somebody at work. Not while they're wukking ... Not unless their wife was taken bad ... or they had a child knocked down, or summat ... Here. Gave me this book to give you back. Said he'd read it. Couldn't understand a word. Thanked you for lending it to him, that is ...

(*Takes the book out of his windcheater.* BRENDA *takes it.*)

BRENDA. What's he doing about being out of work?

ALBERT. Doing?

BRENDA. Haven't they gone on strike?

ALBERT (*laughs*). Nay. It's more of a godsend, really. He gets the same money for doing nowt ... I'm hoping they'll close down all on t'rest. Be all of us on unemployment pay ... Can race me pigeons.

BRENDA. God.

ALBERT. Ever wukked in a factory, have you?

BRENDA. No. I never have.

ALBERT. Till you have I'd mek no comment ... I mean that ... Remember when you first met me?

BRENDA. Don't think I do. Beginning to doubt if I ever did.

ALBERT. Couldn't make head nor tail of it ... Not for weeks ... When I told the lads at work they wouldn't believe it. Not till you came down that day ... Remember that?

BRENDA. Why shouldn't I talk to somebody?

ALBERT. In the street?

BRENDA. Where else? If I hadn't have come up to you we'd never have met ... You wouldn't be here ... We wouldn't have known anything about each other.

ALBERT. Nay ... a young woman ... coming up to a man she's never known ... Only tarts do that ... Cloud-cuckoo-land, if you ask me.

(BRENDA *laughs.*)

You'll see. One of these days you'll be going up to somebody ... as'll not respect ...

BRENDA. What?

ALBERT. Your intentions.

BRENDA. You're just telling me you don't know what my intentions are.

ALBERT. You'll find out. Don't worry. It'll not always be somebody who takes ... an interest.

BRENDA. Interest! (*Laughs again.*) Your entire life—do you know what it's based on?

ALBERT. What?

BRENDA. On fear.

ALBERT. Fear. (*Laughs himself.*)

BRENDA. It's a wonder you get out of bed on a morning ... Every single man I've ever met down there ... They couldn't be more accommodating if they'd been manu-factured in that bloody factory ... They even go on strike like a flock of bloody sheep ... Strike ... strike ... strike ... to show they're as mean-minded as everybody else: small, mean, bigoted, cheap, materialistic. When they've got something to strike about, like now ... nothing. Not a whimper.

ALBERT. I'm surprised you've let me in the house.

BRENDA. I'm surprised myself ... I'm surprised, too, that I come to yours. So small ... In everything you'd think worthwhile ... Even those bloody pigeons ... I can see

their fascination now ... Let them go ... free them from
those horrible little pens ... Up they go ... Then what do
they do? ... The silly little sods come back.

ALBERT. They know they're on to a good thing, that's why.
Regular food ... shelter ...

BRENDA. I can just see why you get upset if one of them flies
off.

ALBERT. That's five quid ... ten or twelve quid sometimes ...
And don't worry ... Other people pick them up.

BRENDA. I think the fact that one of them flies off undermines
your entire existence ... Contravenes your philosophy of
life: *nothing ventured, nothing lost.* All of you: you're about
as mean-minded as the people who exploit you. Between
the two of you—I couldn't make a choice.

ALBERT. Didn't have to open that window, you know. If
you'd have shaken your head—I might as well tell you—
I'd have probably gone straight off.

BRENDA. I can just imagine.

ALBERT. No wonder your sisters are like they are.

BRENDA. That's right.

ALBERT. I mean, I've never heard of anything so bloody daft
... This book you gave my dad ...

BRENDA. You better read it.

ALBERT. Psychology. Crikey. What's a 55-year-old workman got to do with that? Do you think he's going off his
nut, or something?

BRENDA. I think he's already off his nut. So are you. Immo-
bilized. Reconciled to that.

ALBERT. People in glass-houses, you ask me.

BRENDA. Why did you come up here tonight?

ALBERT. Brought that book.

BRENDA. Anything else?

ALBERT. Dunno ... Thought I might see you.

BRENDA. Then what?

ALBERT. Dunno ...

BRENDA. Have it off, then, somewhere? Back porch ... Greenhouse. Got a couple of barns out back.

ALBERT. See I shouldn't have come.

BRENDA. Better get your bike.

ALBERT. Perhaps I better.

BRENDA. On to a good thing, then? ... Your mates: think you're on to a good thing, do they?

ALBERT. How do you undo this catch?

BRENDA. A workman. Should manage a simple thing like that.

(ALBERT *does so, releasing french window: looks back.*)

ALBERT. Well, then ... Better say good night.

BRENDA. Yes. Good night.

ALBERT. I'm sorry you have to be like that.

BRENDA. Yeh ... Sorry.

ALBERT. Well, then.

BRENDA. Thanks for the book. Should have kept it. Told him he could.

ALBERT. Yeh. Well ...

BRENDA. Not beholden. Understand exactly. Well, then, love. Good night.

ALBERT. Aye. Well ... Good night.

(*Gazes at her.* BRENDA *has already turned away.*)

BRENDA. I should go. There's a terrible draught.

ALBERT. Yeh ... Well ... Good night.

(*Gazes at her hopelessly: goes.*

BRENDA *searches round: gets a cigarette from mantelpiece. Lights it. Goes to the dresser. Pours another drink.*

WENDY *comes in. She's dressed in a housecoat.*)

WENDY. Pour one out for me, then, lovey?

BRENDA. What ... (*Swings round, startled.*)

WENDY. Touch of soda ... Not used to it without.

BRENDA. I thought you'd gone to bed.

WENDY. Heard voices ... Didn't intrude. (*Gets her own drink.*)

BRENDA. Listened at the keyhole.

WENDY. Heard a few of the last refrains ... Why not give up the revolution? See exactly how it is.

BRENDA. Why don't you go to bed? (*Flounces across room: sits down.*)

WENDY. What's his name?

BRENDA. Mind your own bloody business.

(WENDY *makes herself comfortable in a chair near the fire.*)

WENDY. Have you ever met anyone you didn't despise?

BRENDA. Not round here: don't think I have. (*She waits.*) Why do you stay here, Wendy?

WENDY. Stay?

BRENDA. Why don't you go away? Get off. Do anything ... Clear out.

WENDY. Don't know ... Used to worry about it, a bit, myself ... Doesn't seem a problem any more.

BRENDA. You ought to be a nun.

WENDY. Could almost say I am.

BRENDA. Why has Jenny never married?

WENDY. Don't know.

BRENDA. I'm beginning to feel the same. Don't think I ever will.

WENDY. No?

BRENDA (*commenting*). Don't sound surprised.

WENDY. Surprised at nothing, love, in this house. (*Gets out a cigarette and lights it.*) Rail all night at the old man drinking ... come midnight, and down she comes herself.

BRENDA. I feel at times we already are.

WENDY. What?

BRENDA. Married.

(*Pauses: gazes at her.*)

I think I'll go to bed.

31

WENDY. That's right ... I'll lock up for you ... (*Stubs out her half-smoked cigarette.*) Leave it to the eldest.

BRENDA. Thanks.

WENDY. I suppose you're more like me than Jenny.

BRENDA. I don't think I'm like anyone. Not anyone here, at least ... Want the light? (*Has gone to the door.*)

WENDY. No thanks.

BRENDA. 'Night ... (*Looks over at the dresser; turns off the light: goes.*)

    (WENDY *sits in the firelight. She lights another cigarette. Smokes. Drinks. Abstracted.*

    Pause.

    Click of the window.

    WENDY *swings round in the chair.*

    Moment later french window is pushed quietly back. Figure comes inside.)

WENDY. What ... ?

    (*She gets up: switches on the light.*)

ARTHUR. Good grief! Jumped out of me bloody skin ... Light went off. Thought you'd gone to bed.

WENDY. What are you doing coming in like this?

    (ARTHUR *is a young man of twenty-one or two, pale, slender-featured: he's somewhat roughly dressed.*)

ARTHUR. Got here earlier than expected ... Didn't want to wake the family ... Been out there half an hour ... Did you know our Brenda's been consorting with a feller? Tripped over his bloody bike ... Half frightened him to bloody death ... Won't come back. Not for a long time ... Here. (*Goes to the dresser: gets a drink.*) Life-saver. By God. Needed that ... (*Coughs: shakes his head.*) Well, then ... (*Looks round.*) How's our eldest?

WENDY. Surviving.

ARTHUR. Not got wedded yet?

WENDY. Not yet.

ARTHUR. Won't have you? Or can't afford it?

WENDY. Bit o' both, I should imagine.

ARTHUR (*looks around him, holding glass*). Nowt changed in here, then, has it?

WENDY. Not much.

ARTHUR. Thought I'd trip in ... Postpone the usual felicitations ... Could see the old man's face ... woken up at midnight.

WENDY. As a matter of fact the front door's still open.

ARTHUR. Well, I'll be damned ...

WENDY. I thought you might be coming this evening.

ARTHUR. What?

WENDY. The phone rang earlier on ... Picked it up. No answer ... Thought it might be you.

ARTHUR. Not me.

WENDY. Run out of coppers ... or whatever it is they use.

ARTHUR. Not me ... Thought if I couldn't break in, I'd use the barn ...

WENDY. Slept there many a time before.

ARTHUR. I have.

(*Pause. Sudden tension between them. Then:*)

Exploited all me native craft for nothing.

WENDY. That's right.

ARTHUR. Fancy one of these? Or are we rationed?

WENDY. Help yourself. (*Turns away: lights cigarette.*)

(ARTHUR *pours amother drink:* WENDY *turns towards him: finds him gazing at her.*)

Oh ... Sorry.

ARTHUR. Ta ... Run out.

(*Takes cigarette from her.* WENDY *holds lighter for him.*)

Lovely ... (*Blows out cloud of smoke.*)

WENDY. Well, then ... (*Waits: watches him.*)

ARTHUR. Damn freezing out there ...

WENDY. I can imagine.

C   33

(*Pause.*)

ARTHUR. Jenny here as well, then?

WENDY. That's right.

ARTHUR. Home from home ... (*Pause. He looks up, overhead.*) Can sense any foreign element in this house ... I remember him lying sozzled there one night ... been comatose for about twelve hours ... Came creeping in ... Heard him call out ... '*Don't worry: I can hear you.*' Dead to the bloody world apart from that ... There's a kind of seismograph inside his brain ... implanted there, I should think, from birth ... its sole function is to measure the proximity, or otherwise, of his only son ... (*Pours from the bottle: nearly empty.*) It can't be the only one he's got.

WENDY. That's his showpiece.

ARTHUR. Showpiece?

WENDY. Doctor's orders ... He came over funny in the fields ... About a month back ...

ARTHUR. Stinking bloody drunk.

WENDY. I think *he* thought the same, at first ... Had a stroke, as a matter of fact ... Has bottles, I should imagine, all around the fields ... Secreted in the roots of trees ... gateposts ... potato pies ... hedge bottoms ... That one's to show he's sticking to his ration. (*She watches him.*)

ARTHUR. Poor old sod.

(*They're silent. Then:*)

WENDY. What've you come back for, then, Arthur?

ARTHUR. Didn't mention it in me letter ... Thought I'd deliver it by hand.

WENDY. Going to prison?

ARTHUR. No. (*Laughs: shakes his head.*)

(*Pause.*)

WENDY. Finish him off, then, will it? ... Or just another jab?

ARTHUR. Neither, really ... Uplift, I'd imagine ...

WENDY. Well, then.

ARTHUR. Getting married. (*Pours last of the bottle into his glass.*)

WENDY. Good God.

ARTHUR. What I said.

WENDY. Who is she?

ARTHUR. Might like her.

WENDY. Hope so.

ARTHUR. An actress.

WENDY. Actress.

ARTHUR. Well ... (*Looks at his glass.*)

WENDY. Go on.

ARTHUR. She was at one time.

WENDY. Older than you?

ARTHUR. A bit.

WENDY. Older than me?

ARTHUR. Bit.

WENDY. Not ... older than Mother?

ARTHUR. Not that bad yet.

WENDY. How old is she? ... (*Shakes her head.*) Not that it makes any difference ... Seem to have age on the brain in this house. (*Turns away.*)

ARTHUR. She's over forty.

WENDY. Forty ... (*Watches him. Then:*) Don't know why you bothered ... Coming to tell them here, I mean ... A letter might have been ... as good.

ARTHUR. She's come up with me, as a matter of fact.

WENDY. What?

ARTHUR. Not out here. (*Laughs.*) In town ... Booked her in ... I thought ... Introduce her in the morning ...

WENDY. Why didn't you stay with her, then?

ARTHUR. No money.

WENDY. I see.

ARTHUR. I'm paying ... For this hotel ... It was the condition I made when she asked to come ... Would have had to come at some time, anyway ... I'd enough for the train fare ... And for one night, you see, at this hotel.

WENDY. Why didn't you bring her straight up here?

ARTHUR. I thought I ought to tell them first.

WENDY. Mad.

ARTHUR. Any more of this, then, is there? (*Indicates empty bottle.*)

WENDY. Ought to celebrate, I suppose. Bit late ... (*Opens cupboard in dresser.*) Doesn't know he has this one, you see. Me mother's been keeping it, in reserve ... I suppose, if she's over forty, she's been married once or twice before.

ARTHUR. Yeh.

> (WENDY *waits.* ARTHUR *looks up.*)

Once ... She's got two kiddies.

WENDY. A father quicker than you thought.

ARTHUR. Yeh ...

WENDY. Not much younger than you ... her children?

ARTHUR. Not really. No.

WENDY. Funny having children ... what? ... almost older than yourself.

ARTHUR. Yeh.

WENDY. Could probably give you some advice.

ARTHUR. Yeh ...

> (*Having got the bottle and opened it* WENDY *pours a drop into his glass.*)

WENDY. I shouldn't have any more ...

ARTHUR. No.

WENDY. If you want to present it all, that is, tomorrow ... (*Waits.*) Is she divorced: or a widow, then?

ARTHUR. Divorced ... Her ... husband was an actor.

WENDY. Oh.

ARTHUR. Quite ... Well. I've seen him in a film or two.

WENDY. Famous.

ARTHUR. Not really.

WENDY. Who's going to do the supporting, Arthur?

ARTHUR. I thought I'd get a job.

WENDY. Good God. (*Gestures up.*) Going to cheer him up no end ...

ARTHUR. Yeh.

WENDY. Does she work as well?

ARTHUR. Yeh ... sort of.

(*Pause.*

WENDY *watches him.*)

WENDY. Do you want another cigarette?

ARTHUR. Wouldn't mind.

(*He takes one: she lights it.*)

WENDY. Three people to support, and until now you haven't been able to support yourself.

ARTHUR. Quite an adventure.

WENDY. Do you still write poetry, then?

ARTHUR. Yeh ... (*Shrugs.*)

(WENDY *gazes at him.*

They're silent.)

WENDY. How long ... (*Gestures at his hands.*)

ARTHUR. What?

WENDY. Have your hands been shaking?

ARTHUR (*looks at them: shakes his head*). Shock of being back, I reckon.

WENDY. Do you feel all right?

ARTHUR. Yeh.

WENDY. If you really wanted to do all this why didn't you write a letter ... Send a postcard. Anything ...

ARTHUR. Dunno.

(*Pause.*)

WENDY (*watching him*). What sort of woman is she?

ARTHUR. All right ... (*Shakes his head, unable to describe her.*)

WENDY. Are you ill or something?

ARTHUR. I think I'll sleep down here.

WENDY. He gets up before any of us here, you know ...
(*Looks at clock.*) Four hours' time ... You'll be safer, I
should have thought, up there.

ARTHUR. Perhaps if we creep up to bed together.

WENDY. Yes.

ARTHUR. Do you mind?

WENDY. No.

ARTHUR. Camouflage ... Calls out: 'Don't worry: I can hear
you.' Might call: 'All right, Dad. It's only me.'

WENDY. Yes ... (*Watches him.*) Well, then ... Bit late ... To
shut the stable door ... I'll just lock up ... Shan't be a
second. (*Goes.*)

    (ARTHUR *looks round. Touches the furniture, edge of
chairs, dresser. Stands by a chair, worn out, exhausted.*
    WENDY *reappears.*)

    You all right?

ARTHUR. Sure ...

WENDY. Should have had an early night.

ARTHUR. Yeh.

WENDY. Anything you need down here?

ARTHUR. Don't think so ...

WENDY. Another fag?

ARTHUR. Yeh ...

WENDY. Have the packet.

ARTHUR. Thanks. I'll get you one tomorrow.

WENDY. No bother.

ARTHUR. Well, then ...

WENDY. Welcome home, then, Arthur ... Don't look now.
(*Looks overhead.*) I think we'll be all right.

    (WENDY *turns light off.*
    They go.
    Silence.
    Last light slowly fades.)

ACT TWO

The same. Morning.

MRS SLATTERY, *wearing glasses, is working at the desk.*

MRS SLATTERY. Damn! ... (*Crosses out. Works.*)

(JENNY *has come in.*)

JENNY. You ought to have someone else to come in and do all that.

MRS SLATTERY. Can't concentrate these last few days ... Did you have a nice time, then, last night?

JENNY. All right.

MRS SLATTERY. Is Wendy giving you a lift to town?

JENNY. She'll have to hurry ... Walk down to the stop otherwise. The speed she drives, the bus is sometimes quicker.

MRS SLATTERY. I think even this ready-reckoner gets it wrong at times.

JENNY. Ought to have a digital computer.

MRS SLATTERY. That's what I said—He says something different ... What's twenty seven-and-a-half p's?

JENNY. One pound fifty.

MRS SLATTERY (*writing*). Honestly ... It's amazing ...

JENNY. Brenda's where, then?

MRS SLATTERY. Went out ... Heard her up this morning, before your father ... Must have been up half the night.

JENNY. What's the old man doing, in any case, in bed?

MRS SLATTERY (*laughs, still writing*). Bed, love? He's not in bed. He's out. Working.

JENNY. I heard him in his room. Just now. Thought he'd

choke to death. Coughing. Called out ... Said he'd be all right.

MRS SLATTERY. Well ... (*Pausing, looking up.*) His breakfast's been waiting half an hour ...

JENNY. Must have come in through the back.

MRS SLATTERY. I suppose I better go up ... (*Looks up, uncertain.*)

JENNY. Sounded sober.

MRS SLATTERY. Got up this morning ... I thought I heard him going out ... Well ...

JENNY. That's Wendy now ... Want one of us to go up with you?

MRS SLATTERY. It's all right, love ... (*Looks up at her suddenly, sees her concern, then laughs.*) For goodness' sake, I'll be all right.

(WENDY *comes in.*)

WENDY. 'Morning, Mother.

MRS SLATTERY. 'Morning, love.

JENNY. Just discovered the old man's still up yonder.

WENDY. So I heard.

MRS SLATTERY. Is he all right, then? ... We've had his breakfast waiting here for hours.

WENDY. Didn't look in ... Going to be late this morning.

MRS SLATTERY. Who else is up there, then? (*Listens, looking up.*) That's not your father.

WENDY (*glances at* JENNY. *Then:*) Arthur came back, Mother. Late last night.

MRS SLATTERY. Oh.

WENDY. Didn't want to disturb you ... Coming down. Shouldn't be a second.

(*Pause.*)

MRS SLATTERY. Why didn't you wake me? Let me know.

WENDY. Would have done. Normally. As it is ... preferred

40

to do it this way, love. (*To* JENNY) Always been eccentric.
Make allowances, you know.

MRS SLATTERY. Well ... (*Gazes up.*) How late was it?

WENDY. Quite late.

MRS SLATTERY. Does your father know?

WENDY. He might.

(*Sounds of someone descending stairs.*)

Seems in very good spirits ... (*To* JENNY) Arthur.

JENNY. Explains all the preparations, then, last night.

WENDY. Last night?

JENNY. Thought you'd been expecting someone.

WENDY. Lovey ... Since when have preparations of that sort
been necessary to welcome Art?

JENNY. What I thought ... Suspected, even, you'd been
having someone in.

WENDY. Good God. (*Turns away.*)

(*Door opens:* ARTHUR *comes in: gazes at each of them in
turn.*)

MRS SLATTERY. Hello, love ...

ARTHUR. Hello, Mother.

MRS SLATTERY. This is a bit of a surprise, then, love.

ARTHUR. Yes.

MRS SLATTERY. Give us a kiss, then ... Not expecting you
for a few hours yet! (*Laughs.*)

(*They embrace:* JENNY *and* WENDY *move away.*)

Got here last night, then, Wendy says?

ARTHUR. Didn't want to wake you.

MRS SLATTERY. I don't mind being woken, love, for that!

ARTHUR. No ...

(*They laugh, uncertain,* MRS SLATTERY *still holding him.*)

MRS SLATTERY. Did you sleep well, then ... ? I was going
to air your bed this morning.

ARTHUR. No ... No ... Slept very well. (*Coughs.*) Could do
with a cigarette ... Got through all those last night ...

41

MRS SLATTERY. Here, love ... I keep some in this cupboard. (*Goes immediately to dresser.*)

ARTHUR (*to* JENNY). Jenny ... How are you?

JENNY. Very well ... You're looking ... better.

ARTHUR. Yep ... (*To* WENDY) Brenda looked in a few minutes ago ... scooted out ... (*To* JENNY) Seen a ghost or something ...

MRS SLATTERY. Brenda's been in a strange mood these past few months ... Made her mind up to go off somewhere ... doesn't quite know where ...

ARTHUR. Yeh ...

MRS SLATTERY. Well ... (*Having given him the cigarettes she stands gazing at him, pleased, excited.*)

ARTHUR. Hope it's not inconvenient, me coming.

MRS SLATTERY. No. No, love. Not at all ...

ARTHUR. Meant to ... present myself this morning ... Wendy here ... discovered me last night.

(*They gaze at him: he doesn't finish. He suddenly looks about the room*).

Well, nothing's changed here, to any great extent.

MRS SLATTERY. Very little ... Can I get you something to eat, then, love?

ARTHUR. Yes ... I'll ... If there's anything going.

MRS SLATTERY. Have anything you like ... You stay here. I'll fetch it through ... It's warmer in here than in the kitchen ... I don't know why ... that great big stove ... I shan't be a minute, love ... (*Gazes at him, watching, before she goes.*)

ARTHUR. Work today, then? ... (*Gestures*) All dolled up.

JENNY. Wendy is always dolled up these days, Arthur ... As for myself: it's true ... We're on our way.

ARTHUR. Don't hang around on my account.

JENNY. No ... No hurry. Let the dust settle in here, I think, before either of us can relax ... depart.

WENDY. Have you spoken to the old man, yet?

ARTHUR. No. I ... Thought I'd leave it ... Usually finds an occasion to make his presence felt.

WENDY. Sulking in his room, you think.

ARTHUR. I heard him sort of ... wandering about.

(*Pause.*)

Is Brenda all right, then?

JENNY. Didn't she say anything at all?

ARTHUR. Sort of ... 'You're back, then? Break in, or gain legal entrance?' so forth, etcetera ...

WENDY. She and the old man, I think, are very much alike ... despite their frenzied attempts to point out all their differences ...

ARTHUR. Well, she was quite friendly when I was last here ... (*Laughs, scratches his head.*) Forget now when that was.

JENNY. Two years.

ARTHUR. Two years? ... As long as that?

JENNY. Then there was that occasion when my mother met you on that station ... Forgotten where it was ... We never did hear how that meeting went ...

ARTHUR. It went all right.

JENNY. Passed over the necessary, did she, Arthur?

ARTHUR (*looks out*). Window was all frozen up when I woke this morning.

JENNY. Been trying to persuade the old man to put in central heating ... Even offered to pay for it ourselves ... 'Who's ever heard of a farm wi' central heating? The whole thing's a bloody paradox o' terms.'

WENDY. Be wishing he had it now, this morning ... Not often he spends his time upstairs.

ARTHUR. I heard him getting up, you know ... I don't know what time it was exactly ... Opened the door ... put the light on ... Must have stood there for a couple of minutes

43

... I don't know what made him look inside ... Like a damn great bear ... In fact, for a while, I thought I must be dreaming ... Wasn't until he put the light off and closed the door ... and went off down the stairs, that I knew I wasn't.

JENNY. Why didn't *you* say something to him, then?

ARTHUR. I couldn't think of anything to say ... Don't know ... Usual situation ... I thought he was going to speak instead.

JENNY (*to* WENDY). The proprieties observed in this house, at times, astonish me ... Can't understand it when, normally, you'd expect us to be at one another's throats.

WENDY. Not as bad as that, then, surely?

JENNY. It's like one, huge, corporeal mass ... I often dream of it at night ... a sort of animal with seven heads ...

WENDY. Seven?

JENNY. Don't know why. Only six of us at present.

(*Sounds of* MRS SLATTERY *returning. Carries on a tray.*)

MRS SLATTERY. You can have your father's ... it's been waiting half an hour ... still fresh ... I'll cook him something else ... Here, love. Pull up a chair.

ARTHUR. Thanks ...

MRS SLATTERY. Look as though you could do with a good meal, love.

ARTHUR. Don't know ... Been eating pretty well these last few weeks.

MRS SLATTERY. Doesn't seem to make much difference. What do you think, Wendy?

WENDY. Don't know ... Very hard to tell.

MRS SLATTERY. Used to fill him up when he was little. Never changed his shape.

WENDY. Congenital defect.

MRS SLATTERY. Well ... I wouldn't say that.

WENDY. Anything for me?

44

MRS SLATTERY. Oh ... love! I thought you'd had it.

WENDY. Don't worry.Get something ... (*Glances at* ARTHUR.) Shan't be long. (*Goes.*)

MRS SLATTERY. Jenny: you're sure, then, are you?

JENNY. Get me coat ... Need me boots on, I think, this morning. (*Goes.*)

MRS SLATTERY. Well, then ... Like old times ...

ARTHUR. Yes. (*He looks up.*)

MRS SLATTERY. Do you remember? We used to eat here when the girls had gone to school.

ARTHUR. Yes.

MRS SLATTERY. Have you ... done much, since we last saw you?

ARTHUR. Not much ... Worked on a farm, as a matter of fact.

MRS SLATTERY. A farm!

ARTHUR. Last summer ... Had a job in a hotel before that ... Then a chap I know got me a job ... sort of teaching.

MRS SLATTERY. Teaching? Are you qualified for that?

ARTHUR. It was a sort of private school ... Sweated labour, really.

MRS SLATTERY. How long were you there, then, love?

ARTHUR. Oh ... Not long.

MRS SLATTERY. Have you got anything ... Have you got any job at present, then?

ARTHUR. No ... I'm ... I had a poem published.

MRS SLATTERY. Oh ... love!

ARTHUR. A few months since.

MRS SLATTERY. Can we get it? I mean ... buy it anywhere?

ARTHUR. I've brought you a copy ... I left my luggage in town, as a matter of fact ... Thought I'd go back and get it, perhaps, this morning.

MRS SLATTERY. The girls ... or your father ... can give you a lift.

45

ARTHUR. Yeh. I'll ... sort it out.

MRS SLATTERY. Well ... (*Gazes at him with a kind of animal affection.*)

ARTHUR. I thought ... while I was up here ... we might go out.

MRS SLATTERY. Out?

ARTHUR. My dad and yourself ... sort of ...

MRS SLATTERY. Together?

ARTHUR. Yep.

MRS SLATTERY. Well ... That'll be very nice.

ARTHUR. Hadn't you better go up ... (*Gestures up.*) See how he is.

MRS SLATTERY. Yes ... I suppose I better ... I found his bottle empty when I came down this morning.

ARTHUR. That's me, I'm afraid ... Last night ... Came in. Wendy was here. We had a drink.

MRS SLATTERY. Oh well, then ... That's a relief.

ARTHUR. Yes.

MRS SLATTERY. Don't you want any more, then, love?

ARTHUR. No ... I'll ... That's fine. I think my dad's appetite's a bit bigger than mine.

MRS SLATTERY. Yes ...

JENNY (*returning with coat and suede boots*). Well, then ... Nearly ready.

MRS SLATTERY. Are you sure you don't want anything, love?

JENNY. Positive. (*Sits down to pull on boots.*) What I want at present, I'm afraid, couldn't—without a great deal of difficulty—be brought in on a breakfast plate. (*Looks up: winks at* ARTHUR.) Wendy's buttering her toast ... eating up her yoghurt.

MRS SLATTERY. The amount that these two eat wouldn't nourish a mouse. I'm quite sure of that.

JENNY. Love, love is what we need: more love!

46

MRS SLATTERY. Well, I'm sure that's your affair. Can't do anything about that. (*Looks to* ARTHUR *and laughs.*)

ARTHUR. Aye ... Well ... I'll carry it back, if you like. It was very nice.

MRS SLATTERY. No, love. You sit down ... I'll take it ... Better get your father something ... Go up and see him. I shan't be long. Is there anything else I can get you, love?

ARTHUR. No. No. That's fine.

MRS SLATTERY. Well, then ... (*Takes tray and goes.*)

JENNY. Home for good, then, Arthur?

ARTHUR. Shouldn't think so.

JENNY. Did our Wendy know you were coming, or didn't she?

ARTHUR. Last night? (*He shakes his head.*)

JENNY. Storm brewing, I should imagine ... (*Looks up.*) Collecting his weaponry ... Don't seem bothered.

ARTHUR. Get used to it, I expect.

JENNY. Yes.

ARTHUR. I thought I'd stay a couple of days. See how things went.

JENNY. Want a forecast, do you?

ARTHUR. No. (*Laughs: shakes his head.*)

JENNY. Heard about his heart?

ARTHUR. Yes.

JENNY. Might quieten down. Grown more morose, if anything, since it happened ... Oddly absent-minded too, at times.

ARTHUR. Surprised to find you still here, as a matter of fact.

JENNY. Me personally, or all three of us in general?

ARTHUR. You ... (*Shrugs.*) Wendy ... well. Think she'll die here if she gets the chance.

JENNY. Put up the shutters.

ARTHUR. Don't know. She seems content ...

JENNY. Disenchanted ...

47

ARTHUR. Quiescent.

JENNY. Might use that, perhaps, in one of your poems ...
(ARTHUR *doesn't answer.*
Pause. Then:)

ARTHUR. I remember working here with you.

JENNY. Working?

ARTHUR. Stooking ... Harvesting ... Days of yore.

JENNY. Yes ...

ARTHUR. Remember Herbert? ... Blond hair ... moustache ...
fat ... had you in the haystack a couple of times.

JENNY. *Wendy!* ... More than twice. Though she wouldn't
admit it.

ARTHUR. I remember that thin chap better ... Gordon.
Always fighting: squabbling over who should work with
what. Do you remember them fighting about who should
drive the tractor ... ?

JENNY. You laughed so much you were rolling on the floor.

ARTHUR. Never seen anything as funny as that. Never ...
Saddest day of my life, I think, when those two left ...
Never been the same since then.

JENNY. Bone idle: both of them ... Met Herbert, as a matter
of fact, not long ago ... so fat he could hardly move about
... married: seven children.

ARTHUR. Sounds just like him. Used to get me dad drunk
in the back of the barn, then they'd sleep it off together ...
Remember the time they ran away? The old man running
round the cow-shed saying, 'What? ... *What?* ... They've
never!'
(*They laugh together.*)
God ... I enjoyed those bloody days ... Never seemed to
rain ... Can scarcely remember any frost ... (*Quietens.*)
(WENDY *comes in.*)

WENDY. You ready, then, our lass?

JENNY. Shall be. Shan't be a second.

48

(WENDY *watches* ARTHUR.)

WENDY. Told her your good news, then, have you?

ARTHUR. No ...

JENNY. News? What good news is that?

WENDY. Thought he had.

JENNY. No ... nothing.

ARTHUR. I was telling Wendy ... last night ... I might be getting married.

JENNY. Good God.

WENDY. Sounded more definite than that — last night.

ARTHUR. Yes ... Well ... (*Looks up at* JENNY.) I shall be getting married.

JENNY. Well, then, love ... I'm glad.

WENDY. Not told Mother yet, then, Arthur?

ARTHUR. Not yet.

JENNY. Not anyone we know, then, Arthur?

(ARTHUR *shakes his head.*)

Well ... (*Looks at* WENDY: *shrugs.*) Nothing more than that?

WENDY. Brought her with him.

JENNY. Here?

WENDY. In town ... Aren't you going to tell her, Arthur?

ARTHUR. I thought I'd bring her up — this evening ... Introduce her.

WENDY. It was going to be this morning.

ARTHUR. Evening, I thought ... it might be better.

JENNY. Well, then, love. Look forward to meeting her ... Young and pretty?

WENDY. Divorced.

JENNY. Divorced? ... Well, she can still be divorced and young and pretty ... Look at our Wendy here, herself.

WENDY. A little older than me.

JENNY. Older?

WENDY. Two children.

JENNY. Arthur! ... You've not done anything daft?

ARTHUR. Don't think so.

JENNY. Honestly, love ... How old is she?

ARTHUR. I don't know ... Forty ... one or two.

JENNY. Good God.

ARTHUR. I don't know. It's not as bad as that.

JENNY. Laddy! You're barmy! Have you told the old man yet?

ARTHUR. No.

JENNY. Go through the roof ... can just imagine.

WENDY. An actress.

JENNY. Actress!

ARTHUR. I said she *was*.

JENNY. She's retired now, you mean. (*To* WENDY) In expectation.

ARTHUR. She's got another sort of job.

JENNY. Well, love, if it'll make you happy ... (*Kisses him.*) Congratulations, love.

(MRS SLATTERY *comes in.*)

MRS SLATTERY. What's that, then, love? ... Congratulations.

JENNY. He's been telling us ...

ARTHUR. About my poem.

JENNY. Poem.

MRS SLATTERY. He's brought us a copy. In his luggage ... By the way, love. Do you want them to give you a lift to town?

ARTHUR. No. I'll ... go in, later.

MRS SLATTERY. Your father's coming down.

WENDY. Ill, is he? Or recuperating, rather?

MRS SLATTERY. No ... He hasn't felt so well.

WENDY. Since when?

MRS SLATTERY. Since when he got up this morning.

WENDY. I see.

MRS SLATTERY (*to* ARTHUR). You've heard about his heart ...

ARTHUR. Yes.

MRS SLATTERY. I wanted to write and tell you ... I didn't have any address.

ARTHUR. No ... I was ... sorry to hear about it.

MRS SLATTERY. It's only to be expected, I suppose ... He takes no notice ... He has one bottle, but I've a feeling he's got one or two hidden somewhere else ... He wouldn't admit it ... He'd lie himself black in the face rather than admit it ... (*Looks up.*)

(*Sounds of* SLATTERY *coming down.*)

(*To* WENDY) Hadn't you two better be off.

WENDY. We'll give it another couple of minutes ... See the prodigal's welcome.

JENNY. Wouldn't miss it.

WENDY. 'Morning, Father.

SLATTERY. 'Morning.

JENNY. 'Morning, Dad ...

(SLATTERY *has appeared at the door in shirt-sleeves and braces.*)

MRS SLATTERY. Do you want to come over by the fire, love?

SLATTERY. No. No ... It's all right ... I'm all right over here. (*Gets out a cigarette: begins to light it.*) How are you, lad? ... We met afore: earlier this morning. Put me head in his room ... Didn't disturb him.

ARTHUR. I hope you're feeling a bit better, Dad.

SLATTERY. Better?

ARTHUR. I heard about your accident ...

SLATTERY. Accident? ... Oh ... that ... Doctors mek up half o' t' stuff they find: be out of a bloody job if they didn't ... Well, then ... (*Crosses uncertainly: puts out his hand.*)

(*They shake.*

BRENDA *comes in the room; she's dressed in a jacket, unzipped: stands watching at the back*).

'Spect you find it a bit cold up here.

ARTHUR. Cold?

SLATTERY. Been travelling round the south, and so on, your mother tells me.

ARTHUR. Oh ... Yes.

SLATTERY. Got here after I got to bed, I expect.

ARTHUR. Yes.

SLATTERY. Never told me ... Your mother.

MRS SLATTERY. I didn't know myself.

SLATTERY. Tell me nowt in this house ... Run by women. Better warn you. (*Turns away to cough and laugh.*) Here's another ... (*Indicating* BRENDA.) Came up with a drop of whisky half an hour back ... Asked me if I'd need it ... Must keep a bloody stock herself ... (*To* MRS SLATTERY) Didn't know you'd been sabotaged, did you, love? Tell'd me last night I was nothing but a sot ... Comes up with a tumblerful this morning.

ARTHUR. Hello, Brenda ... Missed you earlier on.

BRENDA. Yes.

MRS SLATTERY. Aren't you going to give him a kiss, then, love?

BRENDA. Yes ... (*Kisses him formally.*) Glad to see you back.

ARTHUR. Yeh.

BRENDA. Going to stay for long?

ARTHUR. Dunno ...

WENDY. Well, then, Jenny ... off to work ... Anything crops up—know where to find us ... Well, then. Best be off.

MRS SLATTERY. Drive carefully, won't you? These roads ... That lane'll be covered in ice.

JENNY. A hearse overtook us the other day ... I don't think, until then, she'd appreciated the timidity of her driving.

WENDY. Back-seat exponent ... Never learnt, herself.

MRS SLATTERY. Well, then, love ... Take care ...

WENDY. See you all then, later ... 'Bye, Arthur.

ARTHUR. 'Bye.

JENNY. 'Bye, Arthur ... Think on.

(ARTHUR *nods: they go.*)

MRS SLATTERY. Well, then ... (*To* BRENDA) Where did you get to, love, this morning?

BRENDA. Went for a walk.

MRS SLATTERY. Walk? (*To* ARTHUR) Strange hours they keep in this house.

BRENDA. No stranger than before.

MRS SLATTERY. No ... I suppose it's always been a little odd ... (*To* SLATTERY) I'll go and get your breakfast, love ... I let Arthur have what I'd cooked already.

SLATTERY. No breakfast, love, for me.

MRS SLATTERY. Nay, you'll have something, love, I'm sure.

SLATTERY. Nowt ... Don't want ought ...

MRS SLATTERY. Think I ought to ring the doctor ...

SLATTERY. You'll do no such bloody thing.

BRENDA. I wouldn't mind having something, Ma.

MRS SLATTERY. What? (*Hesitates.*) Well, then ... I'll get you something, love.

BRENDA. S'all right ... No trouble ... Done it often enough before. (*Goes.*)

MRS SLATTERY. She gets more wrapped up in herself, I think, each day ... (*To* ARTHUR) Got a job in an office about a year ago ... The manager came to see us. Didn't want to sack her, but he said she'd been going round encouraging the employees to strike ... not for more money, or anything. Wanted them to take over the management ... (*To* SLATTERY) I think he was quite attracted by her – apart from that ... I think if she'd be less dictatorial she'd attract all sorts of interesting people. As it is ... Well, that's *her* problem, I expect ... Spends nearly all her time now writing ... I read a bit of it once when I was cleaning out her room ... Don't ever tell her I told you ... I've never read anything, well ... so lewd. Not just the language ... Well, anyway ... Good job your father didn't see it.

SLATTERY. Meks no difference to me. Gone their own bloody ways ... Gi'en no bloody attention to me ... Never ... Puts me down with the bloody cows ... telling me that last night, she was. Aye. Well. I better get out ... Mechanization ... get just like the bloody machines out theer ... if you don't tell 'em, direct 'em, switch 'em on, tell 'em when to stop and start, reckon they can't do it by the'selves ... By God: had nothing but hosses here when we first came ... I'nt that right? Bloody 'osses know more about bloody farming than any man you can hire today ... Aye ... Well ... I'll go on out ... Back o' yon bloody barn they'll be — brewing up, I reckon ... (*Going.*)

MRS SLATTERY. Get your clothes on, love, you know.

SLATTERY. Don't worry ... Ne'er gone out i' me bloody undies yet. (*Goes.*)

MRS SLATTERY. He takes some looking after ... Ten years older ... At times it feels more like fifty ... Is there anything you want to do, specially, while you're here?

ARTHUR. No — I thought I'd just ... look around.

MRS SLATTERY. Past haunts.

ARTHUR. Yes.

MRS SLATTERY. What was your poem about ... The one you published?

ARTHUR. Oh ... (*Shakes his head.*)

MRS SLATTERY. Did it have a title?

ARTHUR. 'Evening.'

MRS SLATTERY. Evening.

(*Pauses.*)
Can you remember any of it, then?
ARTHUR. Not really.
MRS SLATTERY. Some of it, then. (*Laughs.*)
ARTHUR. It wasn't very long ...
MRS SLATTERY. Go on.
    (*Pause. Then:*
ARTHUR (*Uncertain*).
    We sat by the window talking, I thought, of love;
    The light fell on your face:
    A frown.
    Mine sat in shadow:
    'A simple division,'
    You said.
    'If you move to my side the sun, too,
    Will fall on yours.'
    'Darkness,' I said, 'like light,
    Moves only up or down.'

    The sun set;
    The light crept up the pane.
    'Blackness,' I said, 'comes always from below.'
    'Warmth rises,' *you* said, 'I know.'
        (*They're silent. Then:*)
MRS SLATTERY. That's lovely, love ... (*Waits.*) Did it sell
    well, then, the poem?
ARTHUR. There are only two or three hundred people buy
    the magazine.
MRS SLATTERY. Well, that's something ... At least, *they*'ll
    have read it.
ARTHUR. Yes ...
MRS SLATTERY. It's not the quantity ...
ARTHUR. No.
        (*They're silent. Then:*)

55

I came to tell you, Mother, that I'll be getting married, probably, quite soon.

MRS SLATTERY. What ... ?

ARTHUR (*joking*). Can't you ever think of me as being married?

MRS SLATTERY. Well, yes ... Of course I can.

ARTHUR. Well, then ... Not as bad as I thought.

MRS SLATTERY. Goodness ... Well, I've never thought ... I mean, I thought you'd take much longer, settling down.

ARTHUR. Struck lucky, I expect.

MRS SLATTERY. Yes ...

ARTHUR. I suppose we're engaged, in a way, already ... I've brought her up ...

MRS SLATTERY. Here?

ARTHUR. I thought I'd come ahead ... I booked her in at a hotel in town.

MRS SLATTERY. What she must think.

ARTHUR. No ... No. I preferred to see how people felt ... rather than sort of springing her on you ...

MRS SLATTERY. Yes.

ARTHUR. I'll ... Well, I hope you'll like her.

MRS SLATTERY. Yes.

ARTHUR. Her name's Alison.

MRS SLATTERY. Alison ...

ARTHUR. Not very fond of it myself ... But then I've never been fond of Arthur, really ... You see: two A's ...

MRS SLATTERY. Oh ... Yes.

ARTHUR. She's much older than me ... She's been married once already.

MRS SLATTERY. Oh.

ARTHUR. Certain similarities, I suppose, between her and Wendy.

MRS SLATTERY. Yes.

ARTHUR. Well ... I ... hope, you know, you'll feel quite pleased.

MRS SLATTERY. Yes ... Goodness. I feel a bit dazed, I think ... I never ... Well, then ... Do Wendy and Jenny know?

ARTHUR. Yes. I told them.

MRS SLATTERY. When do you want to bring her up?

ARTHUR. This evening ... I thought it might be best.

MRS SLATTERY. Yes ... Well, we'll have ... (*Looks round.*)

ARTHUR. Oh, there's no need to do anything special.

MRS SLATTERY. We can't have her just coming in ... unprepared.

ARTHUR. Oh, she's very ordinary ... I mean, she won't expect anything special.

MRS SLATTERY. You'll have to tell your father.

ARTHUR. I suppose he'll be relieved.

MRS SLATTERY. Relieved?

ARTHUR. Well, I imagined that he would.

SLATTERY (*off*). God damn it ... Brenda? Is that you?

BRENDA (*off*). Yes!

SLATTERY (*off*). Got that back door wide open? There's a bloody gale through here.

BRENDA (*off*). Yes ...

SLATTERY (*off*). Well, shut it, for God's sake ... (*Comes in rubbing hands.*) Gonna snow. This time of the year an' all. Thought we might've got through without ... Muffled up to the bloody ears. Wonder they can move at all ... Know when they're bloody well off, they do ... Think it's time, tha knows, I had a drop ... (*Has gone to the dresser.*) By God, then. Look at that ... Hope you don't think I've been at it, missis.

MRS SLATTERY. No. No ... Arthur had a drop last night.

SLATTERY. A drop? Half a bloody bottle ... God Christ: I don't sup as much as that meself.

MRS SLATTERY. I thought you'd had a drop already.

SLATTERY. A drop? A drop? ... God Christ: diluted it, she had. Teaspoon to one bloody pint o' watter ... (*To* ARTHUR) Our Brenda ... don't know where she fund it ... Here, then. Was that all we had?

MRS SLATTERY. No ... There's a bottle in reserve. (*Going to the cupboard.*)

SLATTERY. God Christ ... See what it is, then, lad? See what A've come to ... ? Tek me as an example. Don't come any clearer ... a shining bloody light to them that have the eyes to see ... Here. Somebody's been at this, an' all!

ARTHUR. That's me again, I'm afraid.

SLATTERY. Well. I'll be damned ... Sup more than me. I could have told you ... Not in the house five bloody minutes: one bottle gone, another started ... Bloody good job A came down when I did ... By go ... Been overtaken, love: that's me.

ARTHUR. There wasn't much in the bottle when I had it.

SLATTERY. Much? Half on it, that's all ... Mek me into the bloody black sheep and they're supping it when I'm not even theer.

MRS SLATTERY. All right. Now just get a drop and put it back ... There couldn't have been much in, I know Arthur.

SLATTERY. And I know bloody Arthur ... I know Arthur, don't you forget it ... I know Arthur, now, of old ...

MRS SLATTERY. All right, now. I think we've heard it ...

SLATTERY. Heard it? We've bloody heard it. We've done nowt else but hear it ... all my bloody life ... What's he going to do about it? That's what I bloody want to know.

ARTHUR. Do about what?

MRS SLATTERY. Now that's enough. He's not come home for us to start all that.

SLATTERY. Don't know what he bloody well has come home
for. If it's not to borrow one thing it'll be to see if he
can borrow summat else ... Never done a day's bloody
work. Not all his life.

ARTHUR. I have.

SLATTERY. Not that I give a damn. I don't. I want you to
know that, lad. I mean that sincerely. It teks all sorts to
mek a world ... I might work like a bloody animal
meself ... no reason why you or anybody should do the
same ... T'only trouble is ... them that do the bloody work
get no attention ... them that do damn all get nowt but
bloody praise ... Not blaming you. S'human nature.

MRS SLATTERY. Arthur's had jobs, if you want to know.

SLATTERY. Jobs? What jobs?

MRS SLATTERY. He's worked on a farm, as a matter of fact.

SLATTERY. On a farm! (*Laughs.*) How long for? ... Go on.
Go on. I'm listening.

MRS SLATTERY. He's worked in hotels ... He's even taught.

SLATTERY. Taught? Couldn't teach my bloody flat cap, I'm
telling you ... And that's nothing personal, mind. It's
just a statement of bloody fact ... Thy sisters teach.
Bloody woman's job is that ... Good God. They spend
more time on bloody holiday than they do in front o'
their bloody class ... God Christ: I could teach as much as
they do and still run this entire bloody farm meself.
Single-handed ... no bloody half-baked buggers mooch-
ing round those bloody sheds ...

MRS SLATTERY. Yes. Well, love. We've heard all that before.

SLATTERY. Thinks I'm drunk, but I'm bloody not.

MRS SLATTERY. I don't think that at all.

SLATTERY. Thinks I've got one hidden away.

MRS SLATTERY. I don't.

SLATTERY. Well, you must think I'm bloody funny if I
haven't.

MRS SLATTERY. I think, if anything, you're pleasanter when you're drunk.

SLATTERY. What? (*Gazes at her, uncertain.*)

MRS SLATTERY. There, now ... We've said enough.

SLATTERY. Thy's said enough. *I've* said hardly owt.

MRS SLATTERY. Well, hardly owt is enough for one day, love.

SLATTERY (*pauses. Then to* ARTHUR). Spends all her spare time in town ... Evening classes ... Sociology ... Psychiatry ... *Anthropology* ... Trying to find out what went wrong, lad.

ARTHUR. Wrong?

SLATTERY. What went wrong. In here. This house.

MRS SLATTERY. That's not the reason.

SLATTERY. Thinks I'm bloody stupid. Never read a bloody book in my entire life ... I'm wrong theer. The Bible ... That's t'ony book that's any use.

MRS SLATTERY. You wouldn't think so, to hear you speak.

SLATTERY. Didn't know the meaning of Anthropology when she started ... When she got married she was as ignorant as me.

MRS SLATTERY. Well, at least one of us has made some progress.

SLATTERY. Ne'er see this side of her when you're not here, you know ... When you're not here butter wouldn't melt inside her mouth ... Done sod all in your life ... Whereas me ... worked every bleeding minute ... Never loved me ... It's true. She'll tell you ... Never has ... Idolised you, lad. Been your bloody ruin ... Been my son you'd never have turned out like that ...

MRS SLATTERY. That's not true. You know it.

SLATTERY. Nay, if you don't know when you're not bloody loved, then you'll never know bloody owt. As for him ... God Christ.

MRS SLATTERY. Don't listen to him, love ... As he gets older he gets more like a baby ... You do. I mean that. Every day.

SLATTERY. Aye ... Brought four up. I ought to bloody know ... (*To* ARTHUR) I ought to know about bloody babbies. Brought four into this bloody world.

MRS SLATTERY. Brought four in. But who's brought four up? You've brought up nothing but cows and horses ...

SLATTERY. Aye ... Kept you from bloody starvation a time or two ... Ask Him ... Ask *Him* ... *He*'ll tell you ... (*Looks up beseechingly, raising his hands.*) He knows ... He knows everything I've been through. He's been my one true witness all these years.

(BRENDA *has come in.*)

BRENDA. Is anything the matter?

MRS SLATTERY. Nothing's the matter ... It's just that your father I'm afraid's been out again.

BRENDA. Out?

MRS SLATTERY. Wherever he keeps it ... I don't know. He seems determined to spite himself ... All the care we take. (*To* SLATTERY) Arthur's brought us some news which I thought would have made him very happy.

SLATTERY. News? What news? Theer: that's me ration. (*Has held up the bottle after pouring a second drink.*) What bloody news is that, then, Arthur? Good news, I hope. Something that'll gi'e us all a bit of cheer.

ARTHUR. I'm getting married. I wanted you to know.

SLATTERY. Good God. (*Stands gazing at him, stupefied, glass half-raised to his mouth.*)

ARTHUR. I thought I might bring her up this evening ...

SLATTERY. Don't believe it ... (*Bangs his head.*) Summat matter wi' me bloody ear ... That's better ... Hear nowt straight off, you know, these days ... Getting old ... Ask your mother ... Doctor told her: older than me bloody years ... Life I lead: no bloody wonder. Work I bloody get through.

ARTHUR. Her name's Alison ... I'd like to bring her here, if that's all right.

SLATTERY. What?

MRS SLATTERY. He's heard you right enough.

SLATTERY. How old is she? I hope she's got her mother's permission ... I hope you're not shoving her up here, lad, inside a bloody pram.

ARTHUR. No.

SLATTERY. By go ... I've no great opinion of women much, meself ... what wi' the examples I have around me here ... but this ... She's either been bloody locked up and they've let her out—against their bloody better judgment—or she's run away from bloody home.

ARTHUR. She's much older than I am, as a matter of fact.

SLATTERY. *Much* older? How much older? She can't be so much older, I can tell you that.

ARTHUR. She's over forty.

SLATTERY (*bangs his head again*). I'm sure ... (*Bangs his head again.*) I'm not hearing this correctly ... (*To* MRS SLATTERY) That doctor's bloody right, you know ... A'm fading ... Can't hear ought ... A'm fading bloody fast ... (*To* ARTHUR) If I disappear while you're talking, I shouldn't be surprised ... If you suddenly find yourself looking at nowt but that bloody wall behind me ... don't worry ... Natural processes. (*To* MRS SLATTERY) That's what he told me. It is. That's what he bloody said.

MRS SLATTERY (*to* ARTHUR). Is she quite as old as that, love?

ARTHUR. I can't see that it makes any difference.

MRS SLATTERY. No ...

SLATTERY (*to* BRENDA). Could've sworn he said this
woman was over forty ... Good God. As o'd as your
bloody mother, here, is that.

MRS SLATTERY. Nay, I'm a little bit over that. (*Moves
aside.*)

SLATTERY (*to* ARTHUR). *Over* forty ... ? What's that mean,
then? Fifty? ... *Sixty?* ... She's not a bloody octogenarian,
is she? ... By go ... Be wheeling her in i' a bloody bath-
chair next ... (*Laughs. To* MRS SLATTERY) I alus said he
was off his bloody rocker ... That he hadn't two penn'orth
o' bloody common sense ... By God. Of all his bloody
schemes, that one takes the bloody can. (*To* BRENDA)
Going to end up wi' a bloody daughter-in-law o'der than
mesen! (*Laughs. To* MRS SLATTERY) Better get your
books out ... Anthropology. Psychiatry ... See what you
can mek on that ... By go: set them bloody lecturers by
their bloody ears, will that. Have to write new bloody
text-books ... sithee ... mu'n marry somebody o'der than
his mother, then.

    (MRS SLATTERY *has turned away.*)

    (*To* BRENDA) Well: aren't you going to shake his hand
or summat? ... (*To* ARTHUR) What's her name? Alison?
... Welcome thy new sister ... T'only new un, now, thy'll
ever have.

BRENDA. Congratulations, Arthur.

ARTHUR. Thanks ...

SLATTERY. Aye ... Congratulations, lad. If you've done
nowt else you've proved me bloody right ... through all
these bloody years. He has.

MRS SLATTERY. That's a cruel and a wicked thing to say.

SLATTERY. Nay ... I've suffered enough for it, haven't I?
Bloody immortalised that lad afore he was even born ...
that's been your trouble all along ... Set him up ... Good
God ... Thought he was bloody Shakespeare before he'd

even opened his bloody mouth ... sit him in his pram ...
waiting for him to bloody speak ... God Christ ...
Thought we had a new Messiah ... Believed half on it me
bloody se'n ... When he failed every examination that'd
ever been invented I still thought ... '*Bloody genius is that* ...
Can't go t'same road as everybody else.' (*To* BRENDA)
Sweating i' the bloody fields ... looked over the bloody
hedge one day ... lying on his back ... composing bloody
sonnets ... God Christ. Never twigged it. Not till then ...
Slave me bloody gut out and there he was, twiddling his
bloody thumbs and rhyming bloody moon with June ...
Seen nothing like it. Never have ... Here. Better have
another ... Shocks like that don't come every day, you
know. (*Pours another.*) Nowt else to tell us, then? Better
get it over. Let us have it all at once ... No *compulsion*
about it, is there? ... I mean ... no kiddies on the way ...
Nothing that's going to prostrate us any further?

ARTHUR. No ... (*Shakes his head.*)

MRS SLATTERY. All right ... I think we've had enough.

SLATTERY. Enough? ... The fireworks haven't even bloody
started yet ... Brenda. Better fill a glass thase'n.

BRENDA. No thanks.

SLATTERY. What do you think about it, then?

BRENDA. It's very good news. I'm very glad.

SLATTERY. Can see that ... Bringing a light to her bloody
eyes ... Just look. Going to cheer her up, is that, no end ...
Me likewise. 'Have another' ... 'Don't mind' ... 'Deserve
it' ... 'Know that' ... 'Not at all' ... 'Cheers' ... 'Cheers' ...
'Here's to it' ... 'To it' ... 'Well done' ... 'Well done' ...
'Congratulations' ... ' 'lations.'

MRS SLATTERY. Come on, love. Leave him to it.

SLATTERY. S'all right ... I'm off out meself ... Need me out
yonder ... Indispensable in some parts, if not in others ...
See it through ... always have done ... Shan't turn back ...

Never have done ... By God. Last of the bloody line is that.

MRS SLATTERY. Will you be in tonight, or not?

SLATTERY. In? I'll be bloody in ... Damn it all. Wouldn't miss it. Not for ought ... Is that when she's coming, Arthur? Give her my regards ... Look forward to it. Shall ... Don't worry. Shan't let you down. Sit here. Shan't move ... If you think she'll make you happy ... s'all I want to hear ... Theer ... Glass down ... Shan't have another ... Summat in to toast tonight ... Best wishes ... Congratulations ... Sithee ... not drawing her old age pension yet? (*Rams his hand in his pocket.*)

ARTHUR. Don't think so ...

SLATTERY. Could have helped you out a bit ... Know how much it is? Damn all to live on, I can tell you that ... What're you going to live on, if you don't mind me asking?

ARTHUR. I'll get a job.

SLATTERY. Heard all. No ... Really ... I bloody have ... Not been divorced, then, has she?

ARTHUR. Yes.

SLATTERY. Good God ... (*Waits.*) She's not got any children, has she?

ARTHUR. Two.

SLATTERY. Jesus in his holy heaven ... (*Looks up.*) I hope He's bloody listening. I hope to God that He can hear ... Have I ever done ought to deserve a family ... the likes of the bloody one I've got? ... Have I *transgressed*? ... Have I *overlooked* ... ? Have I *condoned* ... ? Have I sinned? Have I done *ought* ... at any time ... in any place ... Said all this before ... I know ... Maybe when I bloody get theer ... He'll tell me what it was all about ... Won't be long ... Blood pounding ... Fit to bloody burst ... Feel that ... Go on. Like a bloody engine ... Get to bloody work ... Hand

to the plough: never look back. Truest words He ever
spoke ... 'Dead bury the bloody dead ... ' He's right ...
All I've looked for ... *always* ... all I've ever looked for ...
all my bloody life ... (*Goes.*)

(*Silence. Then:*)

BRENDA. I'll go up to ... One or two things to see to.

ARTHUR. Yes ...

(*She goes.*)

MRS SLATTERY. I ... better get these seen to, then ...

ARTHUR. Yes ... Here ...

(*Goes to the desk with her.*)

Sit with you ... Give a hand.

MRS SLATTERY. Yes ... Got to get them off this morning ...
Never troubles to do them ... Well ... (*Starts on the bills.*)

ARTHUR. Here, come on ... What's this, then? ... Get them
sorted out.

(ARTHUR *sits.*
MRS SLATTERY *cries.*
ARTHUR *holds her.*
Light fades.)

ACT THREE

Scene 1

The same. Evening.

BRENDA (*off*). Have you got it?

JENNY (*off*). No. I've not.

BRENDA (*off*). It's somewhere ... It was in your room.

JENNY (*off*). Well damn well go and look ... I'm not following you around, looking for everything you've dropped. (*Comes in.*) God ...

(*Goes to framed picture: examines herself in the glass: looks for comb: dressed smartly: trousers, blouse.*

WENDY *wanders in: book, paper, tosses them down: smoking: dressed in slacks, cardigan; no special effort made.*)

WENDY. Not seen my fags, then, have you?

JENNY (*in picture*). Honestly ... what a house ... Brenda's looking for a ribbon: swears she's left it in my room ...

WENDY. What she doing in your room?

JENNY. I let her go there ... to write ... Sun shines in, she says. Finds it warmer.

WENDY. Wouldn't let that nosey-parker anywhere near my things, unattended ... bet she's got my cigarettes ... Pretends not to smoke, keeping herself clean for the revolution ... and all the time, like a bloody furnace ... not to mention all that bloody booze ... A real subversionist is Brenda ...

JENNY. Acquired it from her dad.

WENDY. What?

67

JENNY. He's a natural burrower ... underminer ... Quite secretive, in fact ... Beneath all that bluster lurks a very mischievous, furtive heart.

WENDY. Don't believe it.

JENNY. Don't want to. That's your trouble.

WENDY. You mean the bottles he's got hidden around ... ? Pathetic ... If you call him a natural subversionist I don't know what you'd call our Brenda ... I've never seen idealism confused with so much self-regard before ... or perhaps that's an essential part of it ... I mean, all idealism, at some point, presupposes a certain degree of paranoia.

JENNY. Weren't they supposed to be here, then, by now?

WENDY. So he said.

JENNY. Not looking forward to it, really, are you?

WENDY. Not really, no, as a matter of fact.

JENNY. Why not?

WENDY. I think he's mad.

JENNY (*lightly, regarding herself again in picture*). I think you're quite envious, really.

WENDY. Think I am.

JENNY. Green about the gills.

WENDY. That's right.

JENNY. He's done a very courageous thing, as a matter of fact.

WENDY. Really.

JENNY. He must feel a great deal for her, or he wouldn't have gone this far. Not Arthur.

WENDY. Depends how much he's getting, love.

JENNY. ?

WENDY. How much she's giving him, girl.

JENNY. That's your answer to everything, I think.

WENDY. That's right.

JENNY. Like living in a shop. Give ... take.

WENDY. Never thought of that before ...

68

JENNY. If it doesn't come across to your advantage —
nothing ... I'd say that was another Slattery trait.

WENDY. Really.

JENNY. You're like a miser ... Store it up ... Accuse Brenda.
My God ... What supreme charitable act are you going
to endow, Wendy, with all your wordly, intellectual
charms?

WENDY. You been at the Scotch as well?

JENNY. Don't need to. Got it all in here ...

WENDY. Indifferent as to who gets a share of it, an' all.

JENNY. Not really ... Pick and choose ...

WENDY. Pick some *I* would never choose ... I've never seen
so many men immobilised by one woman in my life
before ...

(JENNY *laughs.*)

I've seen them waiting for you here ... How many, over
the years, I couldn't recall ... All of them: one thing in
common ... *constipation.* (*Grabs at her stomach and doubles
up.*)

(JENNY *doesn't answer: gets a cigarette: lights it.*)

You're as incapable of making a moral decision as I
am.

JENNY. What?

WENDY. Of committing yourself to anything.

(JENNY *doesn't answer: puffs away, unaffected.*)

Accuse me of an acquisitive instinct where people are
concerned, but you ... you never even make a purchase.
You'll end up in some bloody flat ... house ... tenement ...
inviolate ... At least, when I got rid of Bryan, I got rid of
someone who was only asking to be used ... There was
some common decency, I would have thought, in that ...
Are those my cigarettes? I bloody well knew you'd had
them.

JENNY. Found them lying around.

WENDY. Where you find everything in your life, girl. (*Takes one: drops the packet down.*)

JENNY. Child of nature: what I am.

WENDY. Get here when the old man's gone to bed, 'spect ... might be the best, at that. (*Moves away, lighting cigarette.*)

JENNY. You're not making it any easier.

WENDY. Easier?

JENNY. Saying that.

WENDY. The woman's over forty ... Good God. Either she's a raving bloody lunatic, or so insatiable that she'll take anything she can grab.

JENNY. I wouldn't say Arthur was anything.

WENDY. That's more or less how I would sum him up.

JENNY. You don't always talk about him in those terms ... If anything, I always thought if there was one person in the place to whom you are, in reality, quite vulnerable ... that that person might very well be Arthur ... Used to talk glowingly of his literary gifts, I recollect ... Remember? Typing out his poems and sending them to some magazine ... who sent them back and said most of them were a parody of Yeats ...

WENDY. Think I'll start early, as a matter of fact ...
(*Goes to drink: pours one, holds up glass.*)

JENNY. No thanks.

WENDY. Got it all inside. Forgot.

MRS SLATTERY (*off*). Wendy ... ?

WENDY (*goes to door, calls*). Ma?

MRS SLATTERY (*off*). Is your father down there, love?

JENNY. No ...

MRS SLATTERY (*off*). S'all right, love ... He'll be in his room.

WENDY. More likely in Ten Acre ... Totting up.

JENNY. On the whole, I think he'll behave quite well.

WENDY. Really.

JENNY. You know how circumspect he is with strangers.

WENDY. Not with this one, love, I think. (*Looks up at* JENNY, *who doesn't answer.*) Be my guess, for what it's worth.

JENNY. Think he'll surprise you, then. Give you quite a shock.

WENDY. Give me quite a shock, I think: give himself an even bigger one. (*Drinks.*)

BRENDA (*entering*). Told you. Found it in your room ... (*She's dressed smartly, in a short skirt and a blouse.*)

JENNY. Know where to look, then, next time.

WENDY. No Rosa Luxemburg we're entertaining, Brenda. Just Arthur's forty-year-old whore.

JENNY. Shut up.

WENDY. Do you think she cited him, or what?

BRENDA. So bloody funny. So bloody snide.

JENNY. Look quite excited, Brenda ...

BRENDA. Yes ... I think I am. That's right.

WENDY. I'd love to see Brenda with a gun ... Do you remember when the old man used to go out shooting ...? Brought back those bloody pigeons ... I thought Brenda here would die of fright ... Shock ... Paralysis. Seen nothing like it. '*Just look at their eyes!*' (*To* BRENDA) Remember saying that? ... If she behaves like that with a parasitic wood-pigeon what's she going to be like when she gets the plutocratic bastards up against a wall?

(BRENDA *turns away.*)

I think you look quite beautiful ... Really. I think both of you look terrific ... It's astonishing what Arthur's done for us. I can feel the vibrancy running through the building ... tremor ... tremor ... tremor ... even the house, you see, is beginning to feel excited ... And I know this house as well, I think, as I know anything at all.

MRS SLATTERY (*entering*). There you all are ... Your father's struggling into his suit.

WENDY. Suit.

JENNY. Good God.

MRS SLATTERY. When he tries he can make a very good impression.

WENDY. On whom? On whom?

MRS SLATTERY. On whoever he wants to ... now don't go stirring trouble up. We've enough on with keeping one of us quiet.

WENDY. Shan't say a word. Lips are sealed. Condolence: commiseration: sisterly affection.

MRS SLATTERY. One of us is in a good mood, then, at least ... Is that the time? I thought he said he'd be here by now.

JENNY. Post a look-out ... (*At window*) See the lights ... could blow a bugle. What d'you think?

WENDY. I offered to drive them up but he wouldn't have it. Independence. Wanted to carry in his bride ... cross the threshold ...

MRS SLATTERY. It's not got that far yet.

WENDY. That's what we're all here for, isn't it? ... First family reunion for ... How many years?

MRS SLATTERY. I don't think I'll bother to count ... Brenda, you're looking very nice ... Jenny, too.

(*They look at* WENDY.)

WENDY. I made a special effort ... shook out all the dust ... Even put on some lipstick. (*Looks in picture.*) Wore it last night but nobody noticed ... 'cept Jenny. Jumped entirely to the wrong conclusion.

JENNY. Why did you put it on, as a matter of fact?

WENDY (*looks again in picture*). Don't know ... narcissistic ... instinctive ... a bloody-minded reversion, I suppose. Some common or garden impulse, you can be sure of that.

JENNY. Been battling with her femininity all these years ... Quite suddenly, you see, given in ... Makes quite a change. A vast improvement.

WENDY. Brenda battles with her social ideals ... entirely unrealistic ... I battle with my sense of inferiority in being a woman ... Jenny battles with ... I don't know what she battles with ... lasciviousness ... indolence ... sexuality ... acquisitiveness ... What battle would you choose, Ma? What secret is it that you nurture, down there, at the Workers' Educational Institute? Does a rudimentary knowledge of anthropology, psychiatry, sociology, actually enhance your existence, Ma ... does it take it on a step? Or is it a means of protecting yourself against all your lurking fears and fancies that otherwise might pop out ... in bed ... at night?

MRS SLATTERY. Well, I'm sure I don't go down for that ... And I'm sure we're not going to have a discussion at this time of the night ... Brenda: we ought to have a kettle on ... I don't know if Alison drinks ...

WENDY. Bound to ... Woman her age, disposition ... Can imagine her, in fact, quite clearly.

JENNY. Give a year or two, of course: yourself.

WENDY. That's right ...

BRENDA. I've put the kettle on already, Ma.

MRS SLATTERY. Good girl. You see. Not as helpless as you think.

WENDY. Never thought of her as helpless ... ingenuous ... naive ... She could do a great deal, could Brenda, if she really tried ... Like shooting somebody ... or blowing something up.

BRENDA. Might take a bit of your own advice.

WENDY. I might ... Not sure what tonight is going to inspire me to.

MRS SLATTERY. Brought out a strange streak in you, I think!

WENDY. Bring out a strange streak in all of us, Ma ... Ay up ...

(*Sounds on stairs:* SLATTERY *enters.*)

73

SLATTERY (*entering*). Ay up. Ay up, then. Are we here? (*He's dressed in a suit, fresh-faced, hair combed.*)

WENDY. Good God.

JENNY. Amazing.

BRENDA. Super, Dad.

SLATTERY. That's right. Look a picture: nobody here, then, is there?

JENNY. We're here, I'm afraid, but no one else.

SLATTERY. Come early: give us all a bloody shock. (*Goes straight to the drink.*)

MRS SLATTERY. Should you start on that right now?

SLATTERY. Won't do any harm. Oil the wheels ... You're looking very smart ... Not seen a turn-out like this for bloody years ... By God ... you're at it, then, as well?

WENDY. Lubrication.

SLATTERY. Lubrication! (*Raises his glass to toast, and drinks.*) Eldest daughter! (*Toasts. Then:*) Smoking: don't think so bloody much o' that.

JENNY. Drinking, I gather's, just as bad.

SLATTERY. Do as I say, not as I do. Don't take me as an example—told you that afore.

JENNY. I don't think we ever have, you know.

SLATTERY. Is that a fact? Hear that? Bloody daughter. Live inside your bloody back pocket ... any time you ask for ought: 'No thank-you. Manage by meself. ' ... Look very nice, my dear. (*To* BRENDA) Look like a bloody lass, at last. Almost given up bloody hope ... As for these ... God Christ ... What's matter with a bloody skirt or dress ... ? Look at your mother: couldn't look lovelier than that.

MRS SLATTERY. I think they look very nice ... (*To* JENNY) I think it suits you very well.

SLATTERY. Bloody suits, all right ... Here. One more. Then I'll give it a rest ... S'only food. Quite natural. Meat and drink. Me meats in theer ... (*Gestures off*) ... and me drink's in this. (*Pours.*) Not have another?

WENDY. No thanks.

SLATTERY. Moderation. What I believe in ... Sithee, thy'll not be content, then, till men start having babbies and thy can strut around with thy hands inside thy pockets.

JENNY. Might be a good idea.

SLATTERY. Tell thee thy trouble in a bloody flash.

MRS SLATTERY. We've heard all we want to hear of that ... Is that a car?

(*They pause: listen.*)

BRENDA. Gone past.

SLATTERY. Here ... S'not often, you know, we see a sight like this ... By God. Better get the cards out. Have a hand or two at bridge ... (*To* MRS SLATTERY, *giving hug*) Remember that, then, eh? Gin rummy ... Used to lake that, you know, in winter. Too young, these lot, to remember ... Jefferson came across from Shepherd's Nook and old Morrisey from Temple Bank: took some bloody money off 'em, didn't we? Kept thee alive some weeks on what we won at whist ... By God ... some years it cost us more to keep this bloody place running than we ever bloody well got out of it ... All gone now ... motor-car factory, Temple Bank. Used to be a lovely bloody farm did that. Could pot rabbits theer any day of the bloody week ... go over ... have us a dinner for the cost of a bloody cartridge ... Shepherd's Nook ... municipal bloody housing. Had some lovely bloody fields, had that. Woods ... Did our courting there, remember?

MRS SLATTERY. I remember.

SLATTERY. S'likely not forget. (*Laughs.*) Be our turn bloody next ... where we're sitting ... two years' time: six-lane bloody highway.

BRENDA. Probably be worth it.

SLATTERY. I reckon to you it would.

MRS SLATTERY. If the water's on, I better go and turn it off. (*Goes.*)

SLATTERY. Be dead and buried afore then; I shan't have to worry. (*To* BRENDA) Be your heritage: see what sort of job *thy* makes ... with your computerized, mechanized, de-humanized, antiseptic bloody lot.

BRENDA. It'll be all right ... if it's not used to disadvantage.

SLATTERY. Disadvantage?

BRENDA. To give power to some and not to others.

SLATTERY. Power! Want everything in bloody brackets yon: everything has a bloody label ... think we all ought to run down bloody rails ... S' not worth bloody living ... Mek people in bloody factories next. You see. Bloody laugh. They will. Get rid o' bloody ones like me. Old. Out of bloody date. No good ...

BRENDA. I think it's you who runs on rails. Blinkers: never see anything you don't really want.

SLATTERY. I believe in nowt, don't worry ... I want everything ... to be absolutely different ... That's what I bloody well want ... an endless chain of possibilities ... Look at thy two sisters. They're emblem-atic of the modern age ... Free and easy. Responsible to bloody nowt ... Thy brother's another ...

JENNY. We ought to have invited you to school.

SLATTERY. Aye.

JENNY. They'd be entranced. Could give a lecture.

SLATTERY. Ten minutes in that school and you wouldn't have any pupils theer.

WENDY. Where would you send them, Dad?

SLATTERY. Work. Work's the only bloody thing that's real.

JENNY. I think he means it.

BRENDA. I think he does. I don't see any reason why he shouldn't.

76

JENNY. Good God. I can see now where she gets it from.

SLATTERY. Gets it—anything that's any bloody good, that is—gets it bloody well from me.

BRENDA. That's right. I do.

(*They laugh.*)

MRS SLATTERY (*entering*). It's almost an hour ... just look.

WENDY. Do you want me to go and fetch them?

MRS SLATTERY. I don't know ... (*To* SLATTERY) Do you think she should?

SLATTERY. Nay, don't bloody well ask me. (*Turns away.*) Know bloody nowt.

WENDY. I'll drive down. If I see them coming up I can always follow them back ... They might not be able to get a taxi, and the bus isn't due for ages yet. (*To* JENNY) Is that all right?

JENNY. All right by me.

WENDY (*to* MRS SLATTERY). Do you know which hotel she's staying in?

MRS SLATTERY. No, love ... I've no idea.

SLATTERY. There's on'y two ... Tha mu'n ask at each.

WENDY. Right ... Well. If nobody's any objection, then. (*Looks round.*) I'll see you. (*Goes.*)

MRS SLATTERY. She's a good lass ... Always hides her feelings.

JENNY. Where? Where, though? That's what I would like to ask.

MRS SLATTERY. I'm sure I don't know, love. And why: that's another mystery to me.

SLATTERY. I think it's time I had another. (*Getting one.*)

MRS SLATTERY. You've just had another.

SLATTERY. That was the one afore; this is the one that comes just after.

MRS SLATTERY. I'm putting this away. (*Takes the bottle after* SLATTERY *has poured his drink.*) And don't come following me – or I'll put it where you'll never find it. (*Goes.*)

SLATTERY (*calls*). And I've fund it in *that* damn place afore! (*Laughs. Then, to* JENNY) Means the dustbin. Been rooting in there, I have, a time or two. Pour it down the sink, 'cept she's too appreciative of the cost ... If she thought the tractors could use it she'd pour it all in theer instead.

JENNY. You're in a very cheerful mood.

SLATTERY. I am.

JENNY. What have you been up to, then?

SLATTERY. Up to?

JENNY. This ... euphoria: it can't spring up from nothing.

SLATTERY. It springs up from a hard day's bloody work: that's what it bloody well springs up from ... If you did a bit yourself, you'd know.

JENNY. Brenda?

    (BRENDA *shakes her head.*)

Moods change in here so quickly: can never follow them. What're you so glum about?

BRENDA. Nothing ... (*Moves away.*)

    (JENNY *looks after her: takes out another cigarette. Then* WENDY *comes in, in coat: collar up, headscarf: brisk.*)

WENDY. Is my mother here?

BRENDA. No.

JENNY. She's hiding the old man's bottle, as a matter of fact.

WENDY. Right.

JENNY. Anything the matter?

WENDY. No. (*Goes.*)

JENNY. Well ... as long as we know ... (*To* BRENDA) ... ... we'll be all right.

    (*A door is slammed off: feet run down stairs.*
    JENNY *looks at* BRENDA.
    SLATTERY *has gone over to the fire: bends down, pokes it. Door opens.*

WENDY *comes in: casual, coat unbuttoned, headscarf off.*)
WENDY. Got one of those?
(*Takes a cigarette from a curious* JENNY.)
JENNY. What's going on, then? I thought you were off.
WENDY. The prodigal's arrived.
BRENDA. Arthur?
WENDY. I shouldn't go out ...
(BRENDA *has gone to the door.*)
I shouldn't go ...
(BRENDA *goes.*)
JENNY. Extraordinary ... (*Then:*) And where are you off to, then, old lad?
SLATTERY. Up ...
JENNY. Aren't you going to wait?
SLATTERY. What?
WENDY. I should keep it on, you know ... for a little longer.
SLATTERY. Aye ... All right ... All right. I bloody will.
(*Turns back towards the fire.*)
JENNY (*to* WENDY). Has he come alone?
WENDY. That's right.
JENNY. Good God.
(*Door opens:* MRS SLATTERY *comes in: tense, suppressing.*
They watch her. Then:)
Well, then ... Ma?
(MRS SLATTERY *wanders, aimless, straightening cushions, etc.*)
Is Arthur back?
MRS SLATTERY. Yes.
JENNY. With or without?
MRS SLATTERY. He's come alone. (*Wipes her eyes.*)
JENNY. Here we are ... Dressed up ... Queen of Sheba.
(*Gestures at herself. Laughs.*) What's his excuse then, this time, Ma?

MRS SLATTERY. Better ask him ... He's hanging up his coat.

JENNY (*to* WENDY). No one ever tells us anything, you know ... treat us like bloody yokels ... even the kids at school put on a bloody accent ... 'Art 'a barn up o' moor, Miss Slatt'ry? Wearst t'a keepin' sheep?'

(ARTHUR *comes in.*

Pause. Then:)

ARTHUR. Hi ... (*Moves round a moment, restless.*)

(BRENDA *comes back in.*

Pause.)

JENNY. What's it all about, then, Arthur?

ARTHUR. She decided not to come.

JENNY. Why not?

ARTHUR. Don't know. (*Still wanders round the room, fingering various things, putting them down.*)

WENDY. Has she left already?

ARTHUR. Yep.

JENNY. You mean: she *won't* be coming?

ARTHUR. No.

(*Pause. They look at one another. Then:*)

SLATTERY. Well ... coo-shed time, I think, for me.

WENDY. Oh, no. (*Backs up to door.*) Nobody's going until we've sorted this thing out.

SLATTERY. Nay, there's nowt that I mun add. I've said all I've to say, tha knows, afore.

(*Pause.*)

WENDY (*watches him*). You don't seem very concerned about it, Art?

ARTHUR. No.

JENNY. Did you see her earlier in the day?

ARTHUR. I might.

JENNY (*to* MRS SLATTERY). Did he go into town this afternoon?

MRS SLATTERY (*looks to* ARTHUR. *Then:*) I don't know, love. I've no idea.

SLATTERY. We've gone through all this, tha means, for nowt?

ARTHUR. All what?

SLATTERY. Nay, tha mun look around ... Thy sisters dressed up like they've never been dressed afore ... thy mother dressed up like a bloody bride ... I've even put on a bloody suit mesen.

ARTHUR. Then you'd better take it off, it seems.

SLATTERY. Tha'd welcome bloody that, I know ... The invisible event: the story of his life ... Great bloody things he's been and gone and done ... on'y when you bloody well get theer: nothing but a puff o' smoke.

ARTHUR. Do you think it'd do any good, then ... me bringing her up here?

SLATTERY. Thy invited her ... That's what we're all bloody well waiting for ... That's why we're all collected ... that's why we're all on bloody tenterhooks, you know.

ARTHUR. I changed my mind.

SLATTERY. You changed your mind. *You* changed your mind?

MRS SLATTERY. Nay, well ... (*She's about to speak: she turns away.*)

SLATTERY. Nay, bloody hell. Let's have it out ... I've got on me bloody best suit, tha knows. If I can't hear ought in this, I never shall. It's t'best bit o' cloth inside this house ... it mun hear summat for all its bloody pains ... it's been wrapped up in that cupboard long enough ... (*To* BRENDA) Just smell at that. Preservatives. God Christ: I smell like a bloody moth mesen ... What is it? Some clandestine meeting has t'a had? With your mother and your sisters behind my back?

JENNY. Nay, it's not with me.

WENDY. Nor me ... (*She lights a cigarette.*)

(*Looks to* BRENDA.)

SLATTERY. D'ost thy know ought about it, Brenda, lass?

BRENDA. No. (*She turns away.*)

SLATTERY (*to* MRS SLATTERY). Thy's seen her, missis, h'ast'a then?

MRS SLATTERY. No. (*She shakes her head, bowed.*)

SLATTERY. Nay, sithee. (*To* ARTHUR) Tha mun let it out. If we can't celebrate her bloody coming, we can bloody well celebrate her going back.

ARTHUR. I thought it better she didn't come, that's all.

SLATTERY. And when did you decide on that, then, lad?

ARTHUR. This afternoon.

SLATTERY. And you got in touch by telepathy, like?

ARTHUR. I rang her up.

SLATTERY (*to* MRS SLATTERY). I hope he paid for the bloody call. Though if he explained it as quickly to her as he has to us it'd cost him hardly anything at all.

(MRS SLATTERY *has turned aside: she cries.*)

Thy advised her, then, she shouldn't come.

ARTHUR. I left it up to her.

SLATTERY. And you let us bloody well get dressed up for nowt.

ARTHUR. I've got dressed up, you see, as well.

SLATTERY. Nay, bloody pigs dress up as well as that – to have their dinners in the bloody yard.

MRS SLATTERY. Joe ...

SLATTERY. Nay, bloody hell ... I've said enough. God damn it! If in just one thing in his life he kept to what he said.

ARTHUR. I brought her here ... hoping that time might have changed, if not your character, at least your manner ... It seems nothing's got better ... if anything, it's got far worse. I don't know why I troubled even to think of coming back.

SLATTERY. I know why you bloody troubled, lad, all right

... A soft touch ... Me one foot in the grave, soft-headed ...
your mother—as always—as silly as a bloody brush ...
your sisters more interested in themselves than anything
that bloody matters ... One shove, tha thought, and I'll
be o'ver the bloody edge ... an apoplectic bloody seizure
when you bring this octogenarian in the house ... and the
rest is easy ... Well, I'm stronger than thy bloody thinks ...
It'll take more than thee, old as I am, to get me down.
(*Sits down.*)

MRS SLATTERY. Oh, now. We've said enough.

WENDY. Aye ... I think we better take the war-paint off ...
Brenda: have you any useful commentary to add?

BRENDA. Not really. No.

WENDY. Usually loquacious on occasions such as this.

BRENDA. I think Arthur did quite right. He'd be very foolish
to bring someone —or something—he values, into this.

SLATTERY. That's thy opinion, is it?

BRENDA. For what it's worth.

SLATTERY. That's not so bloody much, I can tell you that.
Minus fifteen quid a week, as near as ought. That's what
it costs to keep her opinions on all and sundry coming out.
A back-pocket orator, our Brenda is. And it's my bloody
back-pocket she does it from ... (*He coughs.*) God Christ ...
He'll get me yet.

(MRS SLATTERY *has brought* SLATTERY *a drink.*
He swallows it down: gasps, coughs.)

MRS SLATTERY. Now that's enough. If anything, I think,
you ought to go to bed.

SLATTERY. My God. Can't you see it, lass? Like all his
bloody poems is that ... God Christ. (*Chokes.*) Tha mun
keep away in future, lad ... Tha mun do it as a favour to
mesen ... I haven't got long to go: I can tell you that.
But I mun go my own road: not with thy pushing from
behind.

MRS SLATTERY. Now that's enough ... *Enough.*

SLATTERY. D'ost think I don't see through all his scheming, then? D'ost think I'm as simple as he makes out? I may be finished ... I may be half-way o'ver the edge already ... but, by God, I'll go in my own good time ... I bloody shall ... (*Gasps, holds his chest.*)

WENDY. Here, Mother, then: I'll give you a hand.

SLATTERY. You'll do no such bloody thing! I'll stand mesen ... (*He rises.*) D'ost think I've lost me faculties, then? (*To* MRS SLATTERY) D'ost see them running the house already? I've gone o'ver the bloody top, then, have I?

MRS SLATTERY. He's over the top in one thing, that's for sure. His allowance for the day. You've been drinking in your room.

SLATTERY. I have ... (*To others.*) Mun think I run on nowt. Been married fo'ty years: it scarcely shows. Young as when I first met her, I mun grant her that ... just as pretty and twice as daft ... I reckon I've done all on t'ageing that's gone on inside this house ... there mun be all on't years shoved on me back ... whereas thee, tha knows ... there's not one of you any o'der than when I first clapped eyes ... (*To* ARTHUR) Thy did quite right. If thy'd brought her back I'd have probably been reconciled. You realize that? When it comes face to face— with her, or you, or you ... with whoever they bring in here—I soon step back ... I don't have a bite. You realize that? All bark ... (*Coughs. Chokes.*) I think you're right ... (*Goes.*)

> (*Allows himself to be led out by* MRS SLATTERY.
> WENDY *sees them to the door: stays behind.*
> Pause.*)

WENDY (*pours herself a drink*). Brenda?

> (BRENDA *shakes her head.*)

84

JENNY. I'll have one ... Art?

ARTHUR. No thanks. (*He shakes his head.*)

JENNY. Perhaps it was a mistake ... Inviting her, I mean, like that.

ARTHUR. Yeh.

(*Pause.*)

BRENDA. I'll go up to my room, I think. (*She goes.*)
(WENDY *offers* ARTHUR *a cigarette: he hesitates, then takes one.*)

WENDY. She's been making placards the last few days.

ARTHUR. ?

WENDY. Notices.

JENNY. 'Promises are contracts that you never keep.'

WENDY. 'Two stones may often weigh as much as one.'

JENNY. 'A sorrow shared is a trouble doubled.'

WENDY. 'It's cynicism that makes the world go round.'
(WENDY *and* JENNY *laugh.*)

JENNY. I even wondered ... whether this woman of yours, Arthur ... actually exists.

ARTHUR. That's right.

WENDY. We'll have to take your word for it.

ARTHUR (*hesitates*). You will.

JENNY. We could ask at this hotel.

ARTHUR. I suppose you might.

JENNY. Did you tell her not to come?

ARTHUR. I left it up to her.

WENDY. Do you know where she's gone to?

ARTHUR. I've a good idea.

WENDY. Do you feel like following?

ARTHUR. I suppose I might.

(MRS SLATTERY *comes in.*)

MRS SLATTERY. Your father's asleep ...

JENNY. That's quick.

MRS SLATTERY. I found a bottle half-empty beneath his bed

... He had that while he was getting dressed ... Where's Brenda, love?

JENNY. She's gone upstairs.

MRS SLATTERY. I was wondering whether I should call the doctor.

WENDY. He's been as bad as this before.

MRS SLATTERY. Once ... There was only once, you know, that's all ... He went out like a light when he reached the bed. I've left him in his clothes.

ARTHUR. I thought, Mother, I'd probably leave tonight.

MRS SLATTERY. Love ... where would you go as late as this?

ARTHUR. There's a train tonight ... I've got a ticket.

MRS SLATTERY. Stay till tomorrow, love. I'd hate to see you leave like this.

(ARTHUR *looks round him: sees the others.*)

ARTHUR. I ought to go ... We were going, in any case ... after we'd been up here.

MRS SLATTERY. Look, love ... if you like, you could stay at this hotel ... If you went tonight ... (*Looks overhead.*) I wouldn't like you to leave him when he's been like this.

ARTHUR. I think I ought to go, then, Mother ... I've arranged to go ... I think I should.

SLATTERY (*off*). Missis! Are ye there?

WENDY. Oh, God.

SLATTERY (*off*). *Mother!* Where is she? ... Where's she gone?

(*A great crash, as of someone falling down a stair.*)

MRS SLATTERY. Oh ... No! (*Goes to the door.*)

SLATTERY (*off*). God damn and blast ... what's happened to these bloody stairs? ... Who's shifted these bloody steps out here?

MRS SLATTERY (*off*). I thought you were asleep ... In bed.

SLATTERY (*off*). At this time of the bloody night? Has Arthur gone?

(SLATTERY *appears at door: gazes in, dazed.*)

I thought he'd left ... I thought you'd left ... Apologies. Spoke out of turn.

MRS SLATTERY (*having followed him in*). Joe ... you better go to bed.

SLATTERY. Bed's for the dead ... (*Calls up*) Can write that on thy board! ... (*To others*) Painting notices, tha knows, is Bren ... 'The longest distance between two people is a frown.' Pinned it up outside me door. 'Sin is the sum you can never add up.' 'Don't cross the road afore you know it's there ... ' I've worked like an animal all my life ... she'll tell you ... He'll tell you. (*Looks up.*) Lived like a bloody animal, an' all ... can't keep up ... did I ever tell you that ... seen nothing like it ... stuck here like a Brontosaurus ... detritus from the past: that's us.

WENDY. Do you want another drink, then, Dad?

MRS SLATTERY. For God's sake, love, don't give him any more.

WENDY. How else are you going to knock him out?

SLATTERY. He wouldn't say no ... he wouldn't say yes ... Just pass him the glass ... he'll do all the rest ... (*Sways as if dancing.*) Take my photograph if you like ... Which side do you fancy, lad? Back view's the best ... good for sticking daggers in ... She thinks I'm gone ... One or two loose nuts inside his head ... she could be right. He's seen it all. I have. He has. D'ost think a Brontosaurus never dies? I've seen animals at night stand on their heads ... horns stick in the mud ... that's right ... pull at the plough ... pull at the cart ... Like a dung-heap is this house ... ever so high ... grow cows and bullocks and geese and hens ... Be-asts ... be-asts ... be-asts for meat, and milk ... and bread ... That's very kind. (*Takes glass. Drinks.*) I think our children, you know, should be in bed ... long past their beddy, beddy, beddy-times ... want my advice ...

She's hardly watered this, tha knows. (*To* MRS SLATTERY)
Take more than this to put me down ... I'll have another.
(*Holds out empty glass.*)

    (BRENDA *has entered.*)

BRENDA. It's like acid, or alcohol ... Remorse. It eats him out.
(*Has gone to help him.*)

WENDY. I thought you were on Arthur's side.

BRENDA. I am.

SLATTERY. Been imbibing on her own, has Bren. Sits in
front of her manuscript, pen raised ... her glass in hand ...
a race, at times, to see which gets there first ... ink to
paper, or glass to mouth.

WENDY. I'll bring you one up ... a big one ... if you go to
bed ... Go to bed and stay there, then?

SLATTERY. How big is a big one, then?

WENDY. As big as you like ...

SLATTERY. I'll give it a try.

WENDY. And no more getting out again.

BRENDA. Come on. Come on, then, Dad ... I'll take you up.

    (SLATTERY *is helped out by* BRENDA.

    WENDY *gets a drink.*

    JENNY *goes to the door: helps* BRENDA *get* SLATTERY
    through.

    WENDY, *having got drink, follows.*

    ARTHER *and* MRS SLATTERY *are left alone.*)

MRS SLATTERY (*regards him for a while. Then:*) Would you
stay the night, then, love?

    (*Pause.*)

ARTHUR (*looks over, helpless. Shrugs*). Yes ... All right.

    (MRS SLATTERY *goes.*

    ARTHUR *is left alone. He goes to the drink: pours one.*
    Looks around at the room.

    Light slowly fades.)

88

Scene 2

The same. Night. The room is faintly lit.

ARTHUR *sits alone in a wooden chair, facing the fire: abstracted, still.*

Pause.

The door's pushed slowly open: MRS SLATTERY *comes in. She wears a housecoat.*

MRS SLATTERY. Arthur ... ? (*She comes in.*) Arthur ... (*She switches on the light. She sees his mood.*)
  I couldn't sleep either, love ... I heard you coming down ... (*Watches him.*) Is there anything I can get you, love?
ARTHUR. No. (*He shakes his head.*)
MRS SLATTERY. There's not much heat in that. (*She pokes the fire.*) Are you sure you wouldn't like something, love?
ARTHUR. No thanks.
MRS SLATTERY (*watches him: looks up*). He's sleeping like a child ... You'd never believe it, after all that noise.
ARTHUR. No.
MRS SLATTERY. He doesn't mean half the things he says, you realize that?
ARTHUR. Yes. (*Nods.*)
MRS SLATTERY. And as he gets older he gets more intransigent.
ARTHUR. Yes.
MRS SLATTERY. I suppose ... it hasn't changed your mind—all this?
ARTHUR. No.
MRS SLATTERY. Well ... (*Waits. Looks up. Goes to window.*)
  I suppose it's cold enough to snow tonight ... (*Looks back at him.*) You never brought that poem.
  (ARTHUR *looks up.*)

89

The magazine.

ARTHUR. I'll send it, if you like.

MRS SLATTERY. I'd like that, love. (*Waits.*) I suppose it's difficult, really.

ARTHUR. Yes.

MRS SLATTERY. Getting them accepted.

ARTHUR. Yes ... (*Waits.*)

MRS SLATTERY. I found one in your room ...

ARTHUR. What?

MRS SLATTERY. I ... didn't want to read it, love ... (*Takes a piece of paper from her pocket.*) I couldn't make it out, in any case ... I was going to keep it, love ... If you didn't mind ...

ARTHUR. That's all right ...

MRS SLATTERY. It doesn't have a title ...

ARTHUR. No ...

MRS SLATTERY (*blinks: examines it*). I still can't make it out ... (*Shakes her head. Looks up.*) In pencil, you see ... it's half rubbed out ...

(ARTHUR *after a while takes it from her. Gazes at it. Reads:*)

ARTHUR.

'What will be left? ... A line of bone
and of the brain
little else but dust and stone ...
the frame
of one thought leading to another ... '
    (*Waits: studies paper:*)
'And of all the things he played—
a father, and the game of lover ...
nothing; except the spot where one limb has stayed
the dust, held back a space
and in the earth a gesture
maybe measures out the trace

of flesh, of blood—a creature
still to those who can
recognize in this the emblem of a man.'
(*Pause.*
They're silent.
ARTHUR *puts the paper down. He gets up.*)
I think I'll go on up.
MRS SLATTERY (*watches him. Then:*) All right, then, love.
(*He stoops: kisses her.*)
ARTHUR. Good night ...
MRS SLATTERY. Good night, then, love.
(*He goes.*
Silence.
MRS SLATTERY *covers her face: silent.*
Light slowly fades.)

Scene 3

A simple wooden table has been set in the centre of the room, the
other furniture pushed back.
Shouts, calls off.

WENDY (*off*). Are you in there?
JENNY (*off*). I shan't be long.
WENDY (*off*). For God's sake hurry up, then.
JENNY (*off*). Has anybody seen my boots?
(*Banging on stairs and of doors.*
BRENDA *has come in, brisk, carrying a tray: plates, cups,*
spoons, etc. Begins to set them out.
MRS SLATTERY *comes in: headscarf, coat, gloves.*)
BRENDA. I thought we'd have it in here this morning ... It's
freezing in that kitchen, Ma.

MRS SLATTERY. I've just been out to the sheds ... your father's not got up, and the men have come in late ...

BRENDA. He's up and about. I've heard him stamping. (*Gestures up: having set the tray down she goes to the door.*)

MRS SLATTERY. Are the girls up yet?

BRENDA. They're coming down. (*Goes. Calling off*) Jenny! ... Wendy!

JENNY (*calls off*). Have you seen my boots?

    (MRS SLATTERY, *having taken off her coat, goes to the door.*)

MRS SLATTERY. Didn't you leave them in the hall, then, love?

JENNY (*off*). Could you have a look?

    (*Pause. Then:*)

MRS SLATTERY. All right ... I'll see.

WENDY (*entering*). I should tell her to come down and find them herself ... *Cow!* ... Lolls around all day like a bloody queen in bed ... God Christ: but it's bloody cold. (*Goes to fire.*)

MRS SLATTERY (*off*). They're here, love. Shall I bring them up?

WENDY (*calling*). Leave them down here, for God's sake, then.

JENNY (*off*). It's all right ... I'm coming.

WENDY. Just look at the time! ... (*Calls*) Jenny! For God's sake!

JENNY (*off*). I'm coming ... (*Call: shriek, off.*)

MRS SLATTERY. Bare foot: you see. (*Coming in.*)

WENDY. Serves her right. Has Arthur gone?

BRENDA (*coming in*). That's right.

WENDY. And never said goodbye ...

BRENDA (*entering*). Don't look at me. (*She is carrying in a tray: steam rises from a tureen of porridge.*)

JENNY (*bursting in*). The only reason they were down here ... is because somebody used them to go out last night ...

MRS SLATTERY. That was me, I'm afraid, this morning, love ... Your father wasn't well enough to go out to the sheds.

JENNY. He's well enough now. He's stomping about upstairs ... Is that for me? Oh, jolly d! (*Sits at table.*)
(BRENDA *is serving porridge into bowls.*)
Coffee? Tea?

BRENDA. Both.

JENNY. Oh, I say, then. Jolly good ... Is that my bowl or Mother's, love?

MRS SLATTERY. I won't have any, love ... I'll have some later.

SLATTERY (*entering*). Hello, hello, hello, what's this? Bloody bre'kfast over, is it? afore the maister of the house has had a chance to eat.

BRENDA. Yours is here. It's out and ready.

SLATTERY. By God. Smells bloody good does that ... (*To* MRS SLATTERY) Aren't'a sitting down, then, lass? (*Waits.*) Nay, I'll not sit down till thy has, love.

MRS SLATTERY. Oh ... Well.
(SLATTERY *holds her chair: she sits.*)

SLATTERY. Arthur's not come down, then, has he?

MRS SLATTERY. He's gone already ...

SLATTERY. Aye, well ... A journey before midday, tha knows, is best.

WENDY. What does that mean?

SLATTERY. Tha mun ask Brenda ... Like 'Sleep before midnight gives deepest rest ... ' Wrote that on me bedroom wall ...
(*They laugh.*)
Thy not eating, Mother, then?

93

(MRS SLATTERY *waits, seated.*)

I'll not bloody start, tha knows, till thy starts, love.

(*They wait.*

MRS SLATTERY *draws a bowl towards her.*

Finally BRENDA *herself sits down.*)

Right, then ... a drop for your mother, Brenda ... let's mek a start ...

(*There's a tap at the room door.*

ALBERT *puts his head round.*)

ALBERT. Hello ...

SLATTERY. Good God.

ALBERT. I've been knocking at the door ... the front door, you see ... I found it open ... I couldn't get an answer at the back.

SLATTERY. Nay, come in, then, lad. Come in ... I've never seen you before, then, have I? ... that doesn't matter much in this house, I can tell you ... Come in. Come in. Tek off your coat.

ALBERT (*to* BRENDA, *who has risen*). I thought I'd just come up, you see.

BRENDA. This is Albert, Dad ... Albert ... this is my father ... my mother ... Wendy. Jenny.

SLATTERY. 'Ow do, lad. Have a bowl. Come on. Sithee. Pull up a chair ... Brenda: get us a bloody cup, then, lass ... Don't freeten him to bloody death ...

(MRS SLATTERY, *however, has got up.*)

MRS SLATTERY. I'll get one. (*Goes.*)

SLATTERY. What's his name again?

BRENDA. Albert.

SLATTERY. Albert ... Thy's a friend of Brenda's, then?

ALBERT. Sort of ... Well. Yes.

SLATTERY. Thy work round here, then, d'ost'a?

ALBERT. Yes ...

BRENDA. In town.

94

SLATTERY. In town ... By God. A bloody big place is that ... Tea?

ALBERT. Well, then ... Thanks. (*Sits on chair pulled out for him by* BRENDA.)

    (MRS SLATTERY *comes back, with an extra bowl and cup.*)

SLATTERY. Sithee, then. Here's a bowl o' bloody porridge ... e't it up ... Put a bit o' bloody muscle on will that ... these bloody town lads ... don't know what a spot o' work is till they come out here ... Art'a set, then, lad? ... (*To others*) All ready? ... 'For what we are about to receive may the good Lord make us truly thankful ... for Jesus Christ's sake ...'

WENDY. Amen.

SLATTERY. Amen ... when I say three ... nay, bloody hell ... they've bloody well begun already ... Reet ... one, two, three, then, lad ... we're off!

    (*Laughter: they start eating.*
    Steam rises from the table.
    Light slowly fades.)